See Here, Private Hargrove

MARION HARGROVE

Foreword by MAXWELL ANDERSON

New York
HENRY HOLT AND COMPANY

For

MICHAELE FALLON

Most of the chapters of this book have
appeared before in *The Charlotte News,*
of Charlotte, North Carolina. The author
is indebted to Carey and Edward Dowd
for permission to reprint them here.

CONTENTS

v

CONTENTS

CONTENTS

vii

CONTENTS

FOREWORD

MAKING my way around Fort Bragg last spring on a private tour of duty I came upon what looked like a holdup in the broad daylight of a company street. A tall, good-looking soldier was being rushed by a little gang of buddies who took money from him with wild cries and fierce expressions.

"What's going on here?" I asked.

The ruffians made way respectfully for me, but gave no reply. They were too busy counting their ill-gotten gains.

"What is this?" I asked.

"Answer him, helot," said a swarthy sergeant, thumbing an evidently unsatisfactory split of the returns.

"This, suh," said the tall soldier gravely, revealing an oratorical Southern accent, "is my holding company, making a division of my monthly pay. Gentlemen," he continued, addressing the pirates around him, "you appear to have forgotten the cigarette allowance."

"You can mooch cigarettes this month, Hargrove," said a soldier who carried a camera. Then he smiled sweetly at me. "We got a heavy investment in this guy," he continued. "Where are you from?"

"New York," I answered, telling the approximate truth.

"Who do you know?" said a large dark Irishman, later known to me as Mulvehill. He looked round at his fellow conspirators. "Maybe we could swindle a deal. Who do you know?"

"Just the neighbors," I said.

"Know any publishers?" asked Mulvehill.

"Why?" I asked.

"This guy's always writing stuff which he hands over to us for security. Want to see it?"

"Why not?" I said.

"I'll get it," said Sergeant Sher, and ran inside.

"He's the custodian," said Bushemi, who carried the camera.

"How did this amiable Southerner fall into the clutches of a gang of carpetbaggers like you?" I asked.

"It's love," said Bushemi. "Three times a year he mortgages his folding and his everlasting soul to raise capital for a trip to see his girl. And she won't even marry him. He's a victim. But if we don't send him to see his girl he can't write. And if he don't write we haven't got a prayer of getting our money back. You see, we're pretty deep in."

"I would not have you think, suh," said Hargrove, "that this swindling of deals is entirely one-sided. I am in the hands of my friends, suh, and they supply me with whatever boons I consider necessary for the sustenance of my soul. Grasping as they are where my money is concerned, they would not withhold cigarettes entirely, nor even Cuba libres or reading matter. In fact, there is probably no soldier in this army whose

FOREWORD

wants are more assiduously looked after than mine. As it says in the Good Book, 'Where your treasure is, there will your heart be also.' And this concern for my welfare increases in mathematical proportion to my indebtedness."

"Hey, did you figure all that out?" yelled Mulvehill.

"I am a sheep in the hands of the shearers," said Hargrove.

Just then Sergeant Sher returned with certain manuscripts. Henry Holt has printed them, and here they are.

MAXWELL ANDERSON.

1. IF FIRST SERGEANT CLARENCE A. GOLD-
SMITH, back in the old battery where I was supposed
to have learned the art of cooking for the Army, ever
gets his hands on this, it will provide him with amusement throughout a long, hard winter.

When he reads that Private Edward Thomas Marion
Lawton Hargrove, ASN 34116620, is giving advice to
prospective soldiers, his derisive bellow will disturb
the training program in the next regiment.

"My God!" he will roar. "Look who's learning who
how to do what! My God! The blind leading the
blind!"

It was once said, Sergeant Goldsmith, by the eminent
vegetarian George Bernard Shaw that he who can, does;
he who can't, teaches.

This, dear sergeant, is my contribution to the Army
and to posterity. Please go away and leave us young
people to our studies.

If I were giving advice to the boys who have already
been called into the Army and will go away in a few

days, I'd sum it all up in this: "Paint the town red for the rest of your civilian week. Pay no attention to the advice that is being poured into your defenseless ears for twenty-four hours a day. Form no idea of what Army life is going to be like. Leave your mind open."

Two weeks from now, you will be thoroughly disgusted with your new job. You will have been herded from place to place, you will have wandered in nakedness and bewilderment through miles of physical examination, you will look upon privacy and individuality as things you left behind you in a golden civilian society.

Probably you will have developed a murderous hatred for at least one sergeant and two corporals. You will writhe and fume under what you consider brutality and sadism, and you will wonder how an enlightened nation can permit such atrocity in its army. Take it easy, brother; take it easy.

Keep this one beam of radiant hope constantly before you: The first three weeks are the hardest.

For those first three—or possibly four—weeks, you will bear the greatest part of the painful process of adjusting yourself to an altogether new routine. In those first three weeks you will get almost the full required dose of confusion and misery. You will be afraid to leave your barracks lest the full wrath of the War Department fall upon you. You will find yourself unbelievably awkward and clumsy when you try to learn the drills and the knowledge of this awkwardness will make you even more awkward. Unless you relax you can be very unhappy during those first three weeks.

SEE HERE, PRIVATE HARGROVE

When you are assigned to your basic training center you'll really get into it. You'll drill and drill, a little more each day, and when the sergeant tries to correct or advise you, you'll want to tear his throat out with your bare hands. You'll be sick of the sound of his voice before an hour has passed. The only comfort I can give you is the knowledge that the poor sergeant is having a helluva time too. He knows what you're thinking and he can't do anything about it.

You'll be inoculated against smallpox, typhoid, tetanus, yellow fever, pneumonia, and practically all the other ills that flesh is heir to. You'll be taught foot drill, the handling of a rifle, the use of the gas mask, the peculiarities of military vehicles, and the intricacies of military courtesy. You'll be told to take your beds into the battery street for airing and then, in four or five minutes, you'll be told to bring them inside again.

Most of what you are taught will impress you as utterly useless nonsense, but you'll learn it.

You'll be initiated into the mysteries of the kitchen police, probably before you've been in the Army for a week. Possibly two days later, you'll be sent on a ration detail to handle huge bundles of groceries. You'll haul coal and trash and ashes. You'll unpack rifles that are buried in heavy grease and you'll clean that grease off them. You'll stoke fires, you'll mop floors, and you'll put a high polish on the windows. You'll wonder if you've been yanked out of civil life for This.

All your persecution is deliberate, calculated, systematic. It is the collegiate practice of hazing, applied

3

to the grim and highly important task of transforming a civilian into a soldier, a boy into a man. It is the Hardening Process.

You won't get depressed; you won't feel sorry for yourself. You'll just get mad as hell. You'll be breathing fire before it's over.

Believe me or not, at the end of that minor ordeal, you'll be feeling good. You'll be full of spirit and energy and you will have found yourself. You'll start to look around and you'll see things to make you proud. You'll find that, although your corporals and sergeants still tolerate no foolishness on the drill field or in the classes, they're good fellows when you take a break or when the day is over.

You'll look at the new men coming in to go through the same hardening period, and you'll look at them with a fatherly and sympathetic eye. They will be "rookies" to you, a veteran of almost a month.

For practical advice, there is none better than the golden rule of the Army: "Keep your eyes open and your mouth shut."

At first, probably, you'll be inclined to tremble at the sight of every corporal who passes you on the street. You might even salute the first-class privates. Then, when the top sergeant neglects to beat you with a knout and rub GI * salt into the wounds, you might

* These two letters are the cornerstone of your future Army vocabulary. They stand for the words "Government Issue" and

want to go to the other extreme. This way madness lies.

Let an old wound-licker beg you, from the bottom of his heart and the dregs of his bitter experience, never to walk up to a corporal you've known for three or four days, slap him heartily on the back and ask him if that was him coming in drunk at three o'clock this morning.

When corporals and sergeants are to be dealt with, always remember this: Make friendships first and leave the joking until later. When it's the top sergeant, it might be best to leave the joking permanently.

It can be very easy to start your military life on the wrong foot by giving your officers and noncommissioned officers the impression that you're a wise guy, a smart aleck. Soldiers, like senators, "don't like for a new guy to shoot his mouth off."

So much for the don'ts. On the "do" side, the most important thing for you to watch is your attitude. As a matter of straight and practical fact, the best thing that you can do is to reason that you are going into a new job. The job is temporary, but while you have it it's highly important.

As, when you go into a new job in civil life, you do your damnedest to impress your employer with your earnestness, your diligence, your interest in your work —go thou and do likewise in the Army. As in your civilian job, the impression is made in the first few

just about everything you get in the Army will be GI. Even the official advice. This book, on the other hand, is *not* GI.

5

weeks. You make that impression, starting from the very first day, by learning as quickly as you can, by applying yourself with energy to each task, no matter how small or how unpleasant it is. You don't get anywhere by buying soda pop or beer for your sergeant.

The one place where your attitude toward your new life will show up most clearly is in the traditional salute to an officer. He can see more in that simple gesture than in anything else you do. If your hand approaches your brow indolently, as if lifted by the breeze, he knows that you still begrudge your sacrifice or that you don't give a damn. Snap it up there.

During your first three or four weeks in the Army, you'll hear a lot of griping. You'll be doing a lot of it yourself. Gripe if you must—the Army recognizes its value as an emotional cathartic—but remember that there's a time and a place for it. Don't be unpleasant about your griping and don't get a reputation as a constant griper.

You can stay out of a lot of trouble by remembering that you are no longer governed by civil law. Your new law, the Articles of War, are important, but you don't have to study it or worry about unconsciously breaking some obscure article. The Articles of War are a matter of common sense. But, if you don't like them, writing home or to your congressman won't automatically change them.

The main things to remember are these: Watch your attitude, do your work, respect your superiors, try to get along with your fellow soldiers, keep yourself and your equipment clean at all times, and behave yourself.

Do these and you won't have any trouble with the Army.

For what happens when you *don't* do them, let us now look into the case of Private Hargrove, U. S. A.

2. BRODIE GRIFFITH, managing editor of the Charlotte *News,* adjusted his ancient green eyeshade and began glancing through a sheaf of copy.

"Always complaining about something," he sighed. "I take you off the streets again and again, I give you a decent and respected job, I keep you at my elbow so that you won't be pecked at by the boys in the composing room. And yet you are always complaining. If you are going through a slack part of the day and are at a loss for something to do, perhaps I can be of help."

"If you are implying," I said, "that I am making conversation because I have nothing else to take up my time, let me clear that up. Let me remind you that of the three hundred or so jobs in this newspaper at least a hundred are mine. I was not cut out for this tortured life I lead."

"Please shut up," he said. "Please shut up and get back to work."

"Surely," I said wistfully, "Fate meant something

7

for me better than pouring my life's blood into a rotary press for a thankless taskmaster."

"Hargrove," he said, lighting a cigarette, "it beats the hell out of me what Fate did mean for you. Dr. Garinger down at the high school said years ago that it didn't write a formal education in on your budget. Belmont Abbey found out that you weren't destined to be worth a hoot as a public relations man for a Benedictine college. The drugstore chain in Washington said you had neither the talent nor the temperament for soda-jerking. And you certainly fizzled as a theater usher. Maybe Fate don't know you."

"May I have a cigarette?" I asked, reaching before he could protect them. "Day after day I work my fingers to the shoulder blades for neither thanks nor living wage. I am the feature editor of a progressive, growing newspaper. What makes it that? My heart's blood makes it that!"

"I would fire you tomorrow," he sighed, "if anyone else could possibly straighten out the chaos you have brought to this office. In the most underpaid brotherhood in the world, you are the most overpaid, two-headed brother."

"I am the most underpaid six-armed Siva," I snorted. "Look at me! I am the feature editor, the obituary editor, the woman's page editor, the hospital editor, the rewrite man, the assistant to the city editor, the commissar for paste and copy paper and Coca-Colas, the custodian of oral memoranda, the public's whipping boy, the translator and copyist of open-forum letters, the castigator of the composing room staff, the guest artist for ailing columnists, the tourist guide for visiting school children, the press representative at barbecue suppers of the United Brotherhood of Plumbers and Steamfitters, the butt of the office jokes."

"Period," said Mr. Griffith. "New paragraph."

"I lead a terrible, turbulent life," I wailed. "I am the man forgotten by Destiny."

"If you will get your elbows off my desk," he said, "the boy can put the mail on it.

"What you need," he continued, sorting through a batch of letters, "is a tour of military service. The Army would make a man of you. I was in the Army in the last war. A top sergeant at eighteen. The Army did wonders for me."

"That's not much of a sales argument," I told him.

"Then again," he said, "if we must take up my whole busy day weeping over your sorrows, let's not burden the Army when it has a helluva job already. Concerning the whole matter, I would suggest that you apply yourself to making up the woman's page right now, lest you come down tomorrow morning and find someone else sitting in your chair. Leave my sight."

"There's not a letter there from New York," I asked, "with my name written on it in a delightfully illegible, feminine, and slightly redheaded hand?"

"Is there ever?" he snorted. "Let's see—" and he went through the stack.

"Well, my lad," he said with faint glee, "at last we're

9

getting somewhere. We know what Fate means for you. You can be happy now."

He handed me a long, white, innocent-looking envelope, addressed to me. The return address read, "Selective Service System—Mecklenburg County Board Number Three."

The President of the United States to Marion Hargrove, greeting!

3. THE BOY ACROSS THE TABLE in the Piedmont Grill lifted both hands and clapped his brow three times. He looked at the clock, then back at his breakfast, then back at the clock.

"Oy, weh ist mir," he moaned. "Two years I've been eating here every morning. For two years yet. So the day the Army is taking me to Fort Bragg, they give me my breakfast and where. Here they bring me! They couldn't make it somewhere without sentimental memories? No! They got to break my heart!"

"My name is Hargrove," I said, handing him a cigarette.

"Mine is Piel," he said. "Melvin Piel. Tomorrow maybe you can make it 'Private' on the front."

"So long as you're healthy," I said, shrugging a shoulder. "It cuts down on the income tax."

"My hay fever," he wailed. "What will I do with my hay fever? In the jungles of South Carolina for maneuvers, with my hay fever! Oy!"

"Finish the breakfast," I told him, "and let's get down to the bus station. We have a rendezvous with Destiny and Board Number Three."

"Just look at it," he said on the way to the bus station, "maybe a posthumous medal my grandchildren will get. Private Melvin Piel, who gave his life valiantly and through the nose from hay fever yet. Sneezing to glory."

The bus station on that morning in July, 1941, was a pathetic picture. Four large groups of boys, reconciled to the grim and gruesome life ahead of them, were bade farewell by wailing mothers and nobly suffering girl friends who had come down to see their loved ones off in a blaze of bathos. It was pretty terrible.

The buses swung out of the terminal, through midtown, and out toward the road to Fayetteville. The boys began to feel better, shouted farewells to startled girls on the street and finally broke into raucous song. Four flowers of the nation started a blackjack game on a suitcase in the back of the bus.

Brother Piel's spirits brightened a little. His smooth voice found its way though the hay fever and emerged in song. "It's a lovely day tomorrow," he sang. "Tomorrow is a lovely day.

"Look at me tomorrow," he said, breaking off suddenly. "Hay foot, Private Piel. Straw foot, Private Piel.

Hay and straw and look at what I've got. Hay fever yet! Oy, what a life I'll lead!

"Maybe what I'd better do when I get there, I'd better tell them I'd like to go north. They could use a good man in Alaska."

"The South Pole is your meat," I told him.

"That's it! The South Pole! Boy, I'm going to love the Army!"

The tumult and the shouting died about halfway to Fayetteville. The boys became quiet and thoughtful.

All was still and restful for the rest of the way, except for a steady murmur from the blackjack game in the back of the bus.

4 A SOLDIER STUCK HIS HEAD through the door of our new dormitory and gave a sharp whistle. "Nine o'clock!" he yelled. "Lights out and no more noise! Go to sleep!"

"It has been, withal, a very busy day," I said to Piel, who was buried with his hay fever in the next bunk.

"It sure withal has," he said. "What a day! What a place! What a life! With my eyes wide open I'm dreaming!"

"It's been a little hellish out today," I agreed, "although it could have been worse. We actually saw a corporal and he didn't cuss us. We have eaten Army food twice and, except for the haphazard way the pineapple was thrown toward the peas, it wasn't horrifying."

"I am broken and bleeding," moaned Piel. "Classification tests, typing tests, medical examinations. I think I walked eighteen miles through those medical examinations. It's a good thing this is July. I would have frozen in my treks with all that walking and exposure. Nothing I had on, except a thin little iodine number on my chest."

"Funny thing about the medical examination," a voice broke in from down the line. "Before you get to it, you're afraid you'll pass. When you go through the examinations, you're afraid you won't."

"I noticed that," I said. "I don't have any special hankering for a soldier's life, but I thought when I was going through the hoops this morning that this would be a helluva time for them to back out."

"The little fellow who slept down at the end got sent back," said a loud whisper from across the room. "One of his legs was shorter than the other. He's a lucky dog."

"I'll bet he doesn't think so," said Piel. "At this stage of the game, I'm glad it was him instead of me."

A dark form showed itself in the doorway. "I told you guys to shaddap and go to sleep. Do it!"

A respectful silence filled the room for three minutes.

"Look at me," said Piel. "Won't the folks in Atlanta be proud when they get my letter! Me, Melvin Piel, I'm a perfect physical specimen."

Big Jim Hart, the football star whom I had known in high school, spoke up. "Don't go Hollywood about it, Piel. Just remember, Hargrove's a perfect specimen too. And just two weeks ago, when we were waiting out in front of the armory for the draft board examiners to get there, he had one foot in the grave."

"And the other foot?"

"That's the one he keeps in his mouth."

"Yessir," said Piel, "the Army makes men."

The discussion was interrupted by the reappearance of the soldier. "If youse blankety-blanked little dash-dashes don't shut your cuss-cuss yaps and get the blankety-blank to sleep, I'm gonna come back up here and make yez scrub the whole blankety-blanked dash-dash cuss-cuss floor with a blankety-blank toothbrush. Now shaddap!"

So we quietly went to sleep.

This morning we took the Oath. One of the boys was telling me later that when his brother was inducted in Alabama, there was a tough old sergeant who was having an awful time keeping the men quiet. "Gentle-men," he would beseech them, "quiet, please!" They were quiet during the administration of the Oath, after which they burst forth again.

The old sergeant, his face beaming sweetly, purred: "You are now members of the Army of the United States. Now, goddam it, SHUT UP."

5. WE ARE NOW SOLDIERS.

This morning—our first morning in the Recruit Reception Center—began when we finished breakfast and started cleaning up our squadroom. A gray-haired, fatherly old private, who swore that he had been demoted from master sergeant four times, lined us up in front of the barracks and took us to the dispensary.

If the line in front of the mess hall dwindled as rapidly as the one at the dispensary, life would have loveliness to sell above its private consumption stock. First you're fifteen feet from the door, then (whiff) you're inside. Then you're standing between two orderlies and the show is on.

The one on my left scratched my arm and applied the smallpox virus. The only thing that kept me from keeling over was the hypodermic needle loaded with typhoid germs, which propped up my right arm.

From the dispensary we went to a huge warehouse of a building by the railroad tracks. The place looked like Goldenberg's Basement on a busy day. A score of fitters measured necks, waists, inseams, heads, and feet.

My shoe size, the clerk yelled down the line, was ten and a half.

"I beg your pardon," I prompted, "I wear a size nine."

"Forgive me," he said, a trifle weary, "the expression is 'I wore a size nine.' These shoes are to walk in, not to make you look like Cinderella. You say size nine; your foot says ten and a half."

We filed down a long counter, picking up our allotted khaki and denims, barrack bags and raincoats, mess kits and tent halves. Then we were led into a large room, where we laid aside the vestments of civil life and donned our new garments.

While I stood there, wondering what I was supposed to do next, an attendant caught me from the rear and strapped to my shoulders what felt like the Old Man of the Mountain after forty days.

"Straighten up, soldier," the attendant said, "and git off the floor. That's nothing but a full field pack, such as you will tote many miles before you leave this man's army. Now I want you to walk over to that ramp and over it. That's just to see if your shoes are comfortable."

I looked across the room to where an almost perpendicular walkway led up to and over a narrow platform.

"With these Oregon boots and this burden of misery," I told him firmly, "I couldn't even walk over to the thing. As for climbing over it, not even an alpenstock, a burro train, and two St. Bernard dogs complete with brandy could get me over it."

There was something in his quiet, steady answering glance that reassured me. I went over the ramp in short order. On the double, I think the Army calls it.

From there we went to the theater, where we were given intelligence tests, and to the classification office, where we were interviewed by patient and considerate corporals.

"And what did you do in civil life?" my corporal asked me.

"I was feature editor of the Charlotte *News*."

"And just what sort of work did you do, Private Hargrove? Just give me a brief idea."

Seven minutes later, I had finished answering that question.

"Let's just put down here, 'Editorial worker.' " He sighed compassionately. "And what did you do before all that?"

I told him. I brought in the publicity work, the soda-jerking, the theater ushering, and the printer's deviling.

"Private Hargrove," he said, "the Army is just what you have needed to ease the burdens of your existence. Look no farther, Private Hargrove, you have found a home."

6. THIS WAS A LOVELY MORNING. We began at daybreak and devoted all the time until noon to enjoying the beauties of nature. We had a drill sergeant to point them out to us. We marched a full twenty miles without leaving the drill field. Lunch, needless to say, was delicious.

We fell into bed, after lunch, determined to spend the afternoon in dreamland. Two minutes later, that infernal whistle blew. Melvin Piel, guardhouse lawyer for Company A, explained it all on the way downstairs. We were going to be assigned to our permanent stations.

The sergeant called off the first list of names and the boys fell out. I heard him tell them that they were going to Virginia. "That's nothing," said Piel. "We're next, and we're going to California." Guardhouse Lawyer Piel smiled happily.

The sergeant began the second list. "Moscowitz! Goldberg! Pinelli! Jones! Smith! Brown—" He stopped short. Then he started looking down the front line, choosing men to fill out the list. I smiled brightly from under my floppy denim cap at him.

"What's your name?" he asked.

"Hargrove, sir."

"Groves?"

"Hargrove, sir."

"All right, Grove. Fall in with those men over there."

I fell in and a corporal led us off down the street. I could feel the California palm trees fanning my face. We stopped at Barracks 17 and the corporal led us inside.

"Do we go to California, corporal?" I asked.

"Naah," he said.

"Where do we go?" I asked him, a little disappointed.

"To the garbage rack," he said. "Double quick." He

thumbed Johnny Lisk and me to the back of the barracks.

At the garbage rack we found three extremely fragrant garbage cans. Outside, we found more. Lisk and I, citizen-soldiers, stared at them. The overcheerful private to whom we were assigned told us, "When you finish cleaning those, I want to be able to see my face in them!"

"There's no accounting for tastes," Lisk whispered. Nevertheless, we cleaned them and polished them and left them spick and span.

"Now take 'em outside and paint 'em," said the private. "White. Git the black paint and paint 'HQCO—RRC' on both sides of all of them!"

"This is summer," I suggested. "Wouldn't something pastel look better?"

The sun was affecting the private. "I think you're right," he said. So we painted them cream and lettered them in brilliant orange.

All afternoon, in a blistering sun, we painted garbage cans. The other Charlotte boys waved to us as they passed on their way to the ball park. Happy voices floated to us from the post exchange. The supper hour neared.

The straw-boss private woke up, yawned and went away, telling us what would happen if we did likewise. He returned soon in a truck. He motioned peremptorily to us and we loaded the cans into the truck. Away we went to headquarters company—and painted more garbage cans. It was definitely suppertime by now.

"Now can we go home, Private Dooley, sir?" asked Lisk. I looked at Lisk every time the blindness left me, and I could see the boy was tired.

The private sighed wearily. "Git in the truck," he said. Away we went back to our street. We stopped in front of our barracks and Private Dooley dismounted. "The truck driver," he said, "would appreciate it if you boys would go and help him wash the truck."

We sat in the back of the truck and watched the mess hall fade away behind us. Two, three, four miles we left it behind us. We had to wait ten minutes before we could get the wash-pit. It took us fifteen minutes to wash the truck. By the time we got back to the mess hall, we were too tired to eat. But we ate.

"There's one thing to be thankful for," said Lisk. "Tomorrow can't be this bad."

On the way to our barracks we met Yardbird Fred McPhail, neat and cool, on his way to the recreation hall. "Good news, soldiers," said Yardbird McPhail. "We don't have to drill tomorrow."

We halted and sighed blissfully.

"No, sir," said McPhail. "They can't lay a hand on us from sunup until sundown. The whole barracks is on kitchen duty all day."

7. IT WAS THROUGH NO FAULT OF MINE that I was a kitchen policeman on my sixth day. The whole barracks got the grind. And it was duty, not punishment.

It was all very simple, this KP business. All you have to do is get up an hour earlier, serve the food, and keep the mess hall clean.

After we served breakfast, I found a very easy job in the dining hall, where life is much pinker than it is in the kitchen. A quartet was formed and we were singing "Home on the Range." A corporal passed by just as I hit a sour note. He put the broom into my left hand, the mop into my right. . . .

There was a citizen-soldier from Kannapolis to help me clean the cooks' barracks. For a time it was awful. We tried to concentrate on the floor while a news broadcaster almost tore up the radio trying to decide whether we were to be in the Army ten years or twenty.

We finished the job in an extremely short time to impress the corporal. This, we found later, is a serious tactical blunder and a discredit to the ethics of gold-bricking. The sooner you finish a job the sooner you start on the next.

The corporal liked our work, unfortunately. Kannapolis was allowed to sort garbage and I was promoted to the pot-and-pan polishing section. I was Themos Kokenes's assistant. He washed and I dried. Later we formed a goldbricking entente. We both washed and made Conrad Wilson dry.

Pollyanna the glad girl would have found something silver-lined about the hot sink. So did I. "At least," I told Kokenes, "this will give my back a chance to recover from that mop."

When I said "mop," the mess sergeant handed me one. He wanted to be able to see his face in the kitchen floor. After lunch he wanted the back porch polished.

We left the Reception Center mess hall a better place to eat in, at any rate. But KP is like woman's work— never really done. Conrad Wilson marked one caldron and at the end of the day we found that we had washed it twenty-two times.

Jack Mulligan helped me up the last ten steps to the squadroom. I finally got to the side of my bunk. "Gentlemen," I said to the group which gathered around to scoop me off the floor, "I don't ever want to see another kitchen!"

The next morning we were classified and assigned to the Field Artillery Replacement Center. Gene Shumate and I were classified as cooks. I am a semi-skilled cook, they say, although the only egg I ever tried to fry was later used as a tire patch. The other cooks include former postal clerks, tractor salesmen, railroad engineers, riveters, bricklayers, and one blacksmith.

But we'll learn. Already I've learned to make beds, sweep, mop, wash windows, and sew a fine seam. When Congress lets me go home, will I make some woman a good wife!

8. I TIPTOED INTO THE SQUADROOM so that the sergeant wouldn't notice that I was wearing fatigue clothes. His voice rang out to me as I passed his door, and I slunk in guiltily.

The sergeant's face showed that he was hurt. "You were on KP again today, weren't you, Hargrove?"

I lowered my eyes and scuffed my toe against the floor. "Yes, sir."

"Oh, I get so discouraged sometimes," the sergeant said. "I try so hard to make something of you and what good does it do? Every time I go through the kitchen I see you in there scrubbing the sinks! How many times have you been on KP this week?"

"Only three times, sir," I said, avoiding his eyes.

"It's disgusting and discouraging," he said. "It's more than one poor sergeant should have to bear. Does Mihalakakos get on KP three times a week? Does Droschnicop? Does even Cookie Shumate? No. What was it today?"

"It was all the corporal's fault, sir," I said, looking around to make sure that the corporal wasn't there to defend himself. "Just because I right-faced a few times when I was supposed to left-face, and I zigged when I should have zagged, and because I forgot and smoked in ranks—and a few other things like that."

"And," said the sergeant, shaking his head sadly, "you just turned around casually every time he ordered

23

'about-face.' And you kept watching your feet all through drill. And you stayed out of step all morning and you took those plowhand strides of yours and walked all over the man in front of you. And you sassed the drillmaster three times. And you generally spoiled the whole morning's drill. Why can't you be a good boy and learn the drills?"

"I don't mean to be bad, sir," I said.

"And that's another thing," the sergeant moaned. "Why must you say 'sir' to the noncommissioned officers and forget to salute the commissioned ones?" He mopped his forehead wearily. "Do you know what the top sergeant told me today?"

"No, sir," I said, twisting my cap and awaiting the worst.

"He said—and don't 'sir' me—that when the battery commander had you on the carpet yesterday you stood there leaning on the table, and you shifted your feet eight times. And you saluted four times during his talk —and when you saluted you gave a European heel-click and bowed. And when the captain dismissed you, you told him, 'Thank you, sergeant' and forgot to salute when you left."

"I remembered it on the way back to the barracks, sir," I explained. "Then I went all the way back to the orderly room and saluted him properly."

"Holy jumping Jehoshaphat," moaned the sergeant. He buried his head in his hands and shook it slowly in sheer desperation. Several minutes passed silently. I knew not how to cheer him up.

"Was there anything else, sir?" I asked in a whisper.

"That's all, Hargrove," he said, wiping great drops of perspiration from his forehead.

"Thank you, sir," I said. I saluted, clicking my heels, and turned to go.

"Hargrove," the tired voïce said, "you're not suppose to salute a noncommissioned— Never mind, Hargrove. Just go to bed."

9. "JUST LOOK AT ME," the exercise sergeant roars in a voice that would go four miles against the wind. "Just look! I weigh two hundred and eight pounds and I'm in the worst physical condition I've ever been in! I ought to be busted for the way I've allowed myself to get fat and flabby! I'm ashamed!"

You look at the exercise sergeant and wonder what he's leading up to. To you he looks like the "after taking" part of a malted yeast advertisement. He could probably lick his weight in police dogs.

His next statement explains everything. "Now I'm going to show you an exercise that's so simple it's almost ridiculous. Even I can do it. Now, I don't want to hear anybody down there admitting he's in worse shape than I am. If I can do it, you can do it—or else!"

He outlines the exercise and you begin wondering

how a contortionist happened to wind up at Fort Bragg. This self-styled "fat and flabby" calisthenics master doesn't have any knees or elbows. You stand there waiting to hear his spine fall apart under the strain, but he comes up all in one piece.

"That's the way I want you boys to do it," he says, beaming cheerfully. You begin to feel your face getting gray and you wonder why a bolt of lightning doesn't come to deliver you from the prospective torture.

"One. Two. Three. Four. Five. Six. Seven. Eight. One. Two—"

The first three or four times are the hardest. After that, you get the swing of it. It's really tame stuff, you decide.

"The next exercise," says the sergeant, "is what we call the quarter, half, and full knee bend. It goes like this." He shows you. When you see it, the corners of your mouth go up in a sneer of derision (unless the corporal is looking). Ho hum, you say to yourself. Why do they take up my time with this play?

"Exercise—one, two, three, four—" Quarter, half, full recover. Your knees get That Tired Feeling after the third time. After the sixth time, you feel your eyes getting glassy. After the ninth, you're floating in space. By the time the exercise is over, nothing matters any more.

The exercise sergeant sighs with bubbling energy and bounces exuberantly on his toes. "Didn't that feel good?" he asks. You nod feebly, expecting to collapse at any minute.

A messenger from the battery orderly room mounts the platform and talks for a while to the exercise sergeant. The sergeant's face falls. He turns to the ranks with disappointment written all over his face.

"Sorry to tell you this, boys," he says, "but we'll have to stop here. No more exercise this morning. All play and no work—you know what that means. You have to take your typhoid shots now."

Before you have marched off the drill field you notice that you still haven't collapsed. In fact, you find to your disappointment that you're beginning to feel good. All limbered up.

I told our platoon sergeant that it was just like carrying papers. The bag is sometimes so heavy to the route-carrier that when he sets it down he feels as if he's floating.

"There you go, Hargrove," the sergeant sighed. "Always looking at the dark side of life!"

10. QUARANTINE HAS BEEN LIFTED for us of the July 17 contingency. If the sergeant wasn't looking over my shoulder, I'd say it's about time. Before our release from isolation, Army style, I was able to get around and swap lies and gripes with every one of the boys in our group.

A little under 100 per cent of them came up with the same account, which reads as follows: "Our battery has the worst food in the Army. We've got the worst sergeant in the battery. No kidding, though, our platoon makes all the others look crummy. Here two weeks already and I haven't pulled KP or had the sergeant jump me a time yet. Don't tell a soul, but I think they're going to make me a corporal." All of which is a lot of hot air.

Actually, they're fighting to get into the mess hall first at every meal. They're gaining weight and tanning where they used to blister. They're sassing their sergeants, who deplore them as the sorriest bunch of rookies they ever sweated over. Every one of them has been on KP at least once. As for being made corporals in the next few days—ho hum.

11. BY THE TIME CONGRESS SAYS I may go home and be a mere civilian again, I suppose I'll be the best soldier at Fort Bragg. At least I seem to get more individual attention than anyone else. Private tutoring, I always tell the boys.

We were at work the other morning learning how to handle a rifle. There's a certain way, I found to my astonishment, to lift a rifle, to put it on this shoulder, to put it on that, to present it for inspection, to put it back down. The Army already has each of these figured out before you're drafted and, although they're polite about the whole thing, suggestions from the rear rank are a drug on the market.

The sergeant was putting us through our paces. To be quite frank, the precise way the other citizen-soldiers were doing their part got me confused. Every time I held the rifle at one place, it would seesaw over and finally wind up with a thud on my best toe. The sergeant was quite patient for a while, but he finally called a halt and walked over to me slowly, clenching his fists desperately to control himself.

"Hargrove," he said with infinite sweetness, "where is the balance of your rifle?"

"This is all the supply sergeant gave me, sir," I said. "I thought it was all here."

The sergeant slapped his forehead and mumbled something furiously under his breath. "Wonder-child," he said, "this [pointing] is the balance of your rifle. I can't imagine why they call it that, unless it's because when you hold the rifle there with one hand, it's balanced." He then went on for a few minutes, explaining a few of the things I had still failed to master.

"Now do you understand it?" he asked, beaming at me with a look made of all sweet accord.

"No, sir," I said.

The sergeant sighed wearily. "Private Hargrove," he said, "right down by the next barracks there's a group of young people who are practicing with rifles for the first time. They haven't had theirs for three days like you have. Run along down there and see if you can keep up with them."

I tried. There was some confusion about the orders, however. At the end of a movement where I wound up with my rifle on my left shoulder, the rest of the detail had theirs on the right. I noticed also that I usually finished a command long before the others.

The sergeant in charge of the detail commenced on this. "You know, Shorty," he said, "you have all of these routines worked out much better than the War Department was able to do them. Where it took them sixteen counts to complete the sixteen-count manual, you always manage somehow to complete it in twelve."

I was still blushing modestly when he called the corporal over. He said something to the corporal, who took me by the elbow and guided me gently around the building to a spot where, he said, the battery officers wouldn't see me drilling and thereby be discouraged.

"This," he said, pronouncing each syllable slowly and distinctly, "is what we have come to call a rifle. R-i-f-l-e. It is used for the purpose of shooting. Primitive man, we are told, did not have a rifle. Primitive man was forced to bring down his supper with a knife, a spear, a stone, a bow and arrows or his own little primitive hands."

I nodded automatically and paid scant attention to all this. I already knew it.

"Today," he continued, "civilization has been improved upon to the extent that—" and he went on and on. After that we began at the beginning of the manual of arms and took each command slowly. The corporal sweated for forty-five minutes.

"Are there any questions now, Private Hargrove?"

I thought for a while. "Yes, sir," I said. "That is, 'yes, corporal.' What use will I have for a rifle? I'm going to be a cook."

The corporal mopped his brow. "Well, Private Hargrove," he said, patting me lovingly on the shoulder, "you'll find use for it. Ha ha. In the first place, you can peel potatoes with a bayonet. And in the second place— if you're as good a cook as you are a soldier—you'll need it every day. After breakfast, lunch, and supper you'll need it to protect yourself from murder at the hands of your comrades in arms."

12. "SEE HERE, PRIVATE HARGROVE," the sergeant sighed. "Can't you try just once to do something right? Don't you want to be a credit to the platoon? You don't want us to be the worst bunch in the battery after we've been the best for so long, do you?"

"Please, sergeant," I begged him, "couldn't I just stay inside for this once? They'd never miss me at rifle inspection. I'd be very quiet and nobody would ever know."

He ignored the request. "Try hard to remember, private, these few simple things. When the officer reaches the man next to you, open the rifle. When he grabs your gun, don't hang onto it or you'll have a bellyache for two weeks. When he throws it back to you, don't catch it with your chin. And when you get it back, snap the trigger. And heaven help you if you ball this thing up!"

The forces of Destiny placed me second in the front rank at inspection. We stood at attention for three minutes before the inspecting officer approached. Four seconds after we brought our rifles up for inspection, a fly which seemed to be a little larger than a June bug landed on my forehead. The sergeant shot a warning glance across my bow and I decided to humor the fly. It would go away soon, I told myself, although I knew it wouldn't.

The hell-sent little beast walked all the way across my forehead and back again. It stopped awhile, wiped its shoes and began pacing back and forth, stamping its feet. Then my nose began to itch.

The inspecting officer still had not begun his rounds. He was waiting for us to get off our guard. The fly demonstrated its impatience by stepping up to double-quick in its pacing. "Oh, if I only had you alone!" I thought. The itching nose became more insistent. A gnat made a three-point landing on it and began playing about the left nostril.

I gave the sergeant a glance which said distinctly, "This can't go on much longer. Something's going to pop!" His return glance said, in italicized words, "Bat just one eyelash and I'll break your neck!"

Suddenly the inspecting officer grabbed the rifle from the hand of Grafenstein, who stood beside me. His lightning swoop on the gun, coupled with the speed with which Grafenstein relinquished it, completely paralyzed me. An almost inaudible groan made me look at the sergeant. He was making furious grimaces at me and his face looked as if he was going to burst a blood vessel. He kept wagging his eyes down to the bolt of my rifle. A split second before the officer reached me, I managed to pull the bolt.

In the fraction of a second before the officer got to me, the little voice inside me repeated again and again: "He's going to snatch that rifle from you about three seconds before you release it. You won't turn loose when he grabs it, not you!" I could already feel the impact as the gun pivoted on my hand and smacked my hip. I could see the sergeant unloading freight carloads of potatoes for me to peel. I could see the next weekend, with me restricted to quarters while the rest of the platoon enjoyed themselves in town.

The officer reached me several lifetimes later. He looked at my face and sighed wearily. Then, with infinite tenderness, he gently lifted the rifle from my grasp. He inspected it and handed it back to me as though he was laying a brick on an orchid or giving a hundred-pound weight to his aged grandmother. He sighed again and passed on to the next man, whose rifle he grabbed with the confidence that the man wouldn't fall apart when he snatched it.

When he threw the man's rifle back, the soldier snapped his trigger. "Heavens to Betsy!" I said to myself, except that I used stronger terms. A cold sweat broke out on my forehead, making the fly walk more slowly. I strained my eyes down, past the tip of my nose, where the gnat played merrily, and down to the rifle. The cocking-piece stood out like a sore thumb.

Another trigger snapped farther down the line, then another and another. The itching nose froze; the fly and the gnat retreated before the approaching catastrophe. I felt my hand straining toward the trigger and I held it back desperately.

My only hope, I knew, was a long chance. On the next trigger snap, I would pull mine at the same time and the two sounds would be one.

I waited my time and when I thought the next man was ready to pull his trigger, I tightened my finger on mine. In the silence, the snap of my trigger sounded like a slap. It could have been heard from one end of the battery street to the other.

Oh, well! The kitchen isn't so bad after you get used to it.

13. SELECTEE JOSEPH G. GANTT, late of Liberty, South Carolina, came out for reveille this morning with a grin you could have used for a foot rule. He held both his arms against the front of his shirt in a queerly strained posture and blushed happily every time someone looked at him.

"The heat's got the boy," I told Gene Shumate. "Looks like the best ones always go first."

"That ain't the heat," said Cookie. "He seems to have a cramp in his arms." We looked at Citizen-Soldier Gantt's arms again. Then, for the first time, we noticed two shining stripes on each sleeve. Citizen-Soldier Gantt was a corporal now!

"Heavens to Betsy," we shouted in unison for his benefit. "Is that punk a corporal?" Corporal Gantt acknowledged the tribute by joyfully changing his color to a holiday red. The grin widened until his ears hung perilously on the brink of his lips. It took him half the morning to sober his spirits to working conditions.

Corporal Gantt has been in the Army exactly four months. He had been an acting corporal for three weeks before he got his stripes.

A nice, quiet, studious-looking boy, the new corporal belies the old legend about Army corporals. The fiction writers and cartoonists will pass him by. He doesn't bum cigarettes from the boys, he doesn't cuss the yardbirds; in fact, he's one of the most popular boys in the battery.

We privates in the rear ranks plan to work on him, though. With a little training, we can make him into a real shouting, sarcastic corporal like the ones in the movies. He's adaptable. Supply Sergeant Israel says that Joseph G. was a boy soprano when he came here. Now he can almost bark his commands on the drill field.

Heaven grant him strength for the ordeal ahead.

The term "buck private" was explained to us this afternoon. It refers to the Old Army Game, "passing the buck." The sergeant is first called on the carpet for a mistake in his platoon. The sergeant seeks out the corporal and gives him a dressing-down. The corporal passes the buck by scalding the ears of the private. The private doesn't even have a mule to kick, so he can't pass the buck any farther. He keeps it. That makes him a buck private. . . .

The Army, I find, has many subtle ways to trap the unwary into volunteering for work. First there was the sergeant over at the Reception Center who came through the recreation hall one afternoon calling for "Private Smith." Four men answered. All four were put to work picking up cigarette stubs.

On the call, "Anybody in here know how to handle a truck?" don't speak up. The last three were seen later pushing a hand truck up the battery street to haul rifle racks.

Corporal Henry Ussery is to date the most dangerous conscriptor. This week he came into the squadroom to ask if anyone was good at shorthand. Three citizen-soldiers admitted that they were.

"Report to the kitchen," the corporal laughed. "The mess sergeant says he's shorthanded on dishwashers!"

14. "ONE OF THE MOST SOLEMN AND RE-SPONSIBLE TRUSTS of a soldier," Sergeant "Curly" Taylor said today, "is his guard duty." Sergeant Taylor, who has been in the Army for nineteen years and probably knows more about guard duty than any man in Fort Bragg, is teaching us about guard duty now.

The soldier is called to this duty about once a month. For a twenty-four-hour period, he is on two hours, and off four hours, and he "walks his post in a military manner," guarding the peace and possessions and safety of a part of the post. He is responsible only to a corporal of the guard, a sergeant of the guard, an officer of the day, and his commanding officer.

The guard, or sentry, is known chiefly to the reading and movie-going public by two expressions, "Halt, who goes there?" and "Corporal of the guard! Post number three!" The former, Sergeant Taylor said with his best poker-face, has given the Army considerable worry at times.

According to the sergeant, the guard is instructed to give the "halt" order three times and then shoot. Over-enthusiastic rookies from the back counties, he said, had been known to go like this: "Halt halt halt! Ka-POW!" (You can believe it or leave it; I never question what the sergeant says.)

There was one rookie guard, he said, who halted him, questioned him and allowed him to pass. After he had gone several steps, the sentry again shouted, "Halt!" Sergeant Taylor came back and wanted to know—politely, of course—how come. "My orders," said the guard, "say to holler 'Halt' three times and then shoot. You're just on your second halt now!"

The other popular expression is the come-a-running call that goes up the line to the guardhouse when a guard takes a prisoner or "meets any case not covered by instruction" (General Order No. 9). If the guard is on the seventh post, he sings out, "Corporal of the guard! Post number seven!" The guard on the sixth post picks up the cry and it goes down the line like that.

There's the story about the officer of the day who questioned a new sentry, as officers of the day frequently do in order to test the sentries. "Suppose," the OD asked, "that you shouted 'Halt' three times and I kept going. What would you do?"

The guard was apparently stumped bv the question.

Finally he answered, "Sir, I'd call the corporal of the guard."

The officer of the day gloated. "Aha!" he said. "So you'd call the corporal of the guard, would you? And just why would you call the corporal of the guard?"

This time the answer was prompt and decisive—and correct. "To haul away your dead body, sir!"

Another promising young guard, Sergeant Taylor says, was questioned by a sergeant of the guard. "Suppose you saw a battleship coming across that drill field over there. What would you do?"

The guard thought furiously. The answer—General Order No. 9—didn't come.

"What would you do?" the sergeant insisted.

A light came into the sentry's eyes. "I'd torpedo the thing and sink it."

The sergeant gasped. "Where would you get a torpedo?" he demanded.

The guard smiled brightly. "The same place you got that damned battleship," he said.

Heroes are born, not made.

15. THERE'S ONE JOB HERE that is nothing but goldbricking in itself. That's the latrine orderly detail. You go to work after lunch and spend the rest of the

afternoon watching the fire in the water heater and feeding it regularly—every two hours. The next morning you sweep and mop the washroom and spend the rest of the time until lunch watching the fire again. All in all, you lead a lazy, carefree existence.

There was a slip-up somewhere yesterday. I was latrine orderly instead of a KP. It was probably the mess sergeant's idea.

The boys started out after lunch for an afternoon of drilling in the warm Carolina sunshine and learning to drive trucks across ditches. "Goldbrick," they muttered as they passed me. "Goldbrick. Now he's going professional." I brushed them away disdainfully and sat down to read a comic book or two.

An hour later, I decided to take a casual look at the boiler. When I opened the furnace-room door, a blast of strong brownish smoke struck me to the ground. I lay there for several minutes, tapping my forehead thoughtfully, while more smoke poured out.

When it still hadn't slackened after five minutes, I crawled under the layer of smoke to the boiler. There the sickening vapor was, pouring nonchalantly through chinks in the door.

"Don't come telling me about it," said Sergeant "Ma" Davidson. "Take out the pipes and clean them. All of them."

I almost dropped. "Clean them smoke pipes? With a fire going? I can't do it."

I had to see the top sergeant to get my instructions.

When I returned to Sergeant Davidson I was happy again.

"Ma," I told him, "the top kick says for you to supervise the job."

The sergeant was furious with rage and frustration. I grabbed a screwdriver and he grabbed Private Downer, who had a black mark by his name for not wearing his identification tag. The three of us started work.

First, put out the fire in the boiler. Shake it down, throw ashes on it. It still burns. Shake it down more, throw sand on it. Still burns. Close the bottom door, shake it down more, throw ashes and sand on it. Curse it. After too long, it dies.

The man who devised the system for connecting an indoor boiler and an outdoor chimney should be parched with his own pipes and stuffed with oily soot.

Unscrew a pipe, lift it gently, coax it from its socket. Easy does it. Careful there. When you have it almost out, inhale for your sigh of relief. Crash! The whole network of pipes bounces off the floor, scattering ashes and soot over half the battery area.

The sergeant's mother in Gaffney, South Carolina, would be amazed to find how her son's vocabulary has improved since he enlisted in the Army. Even for a sergeant, his speech is forceful as he helps to gather up the litter of pipes, screws, and selectees.

After half an hour of scrubbing and wiping the interior regions of all of the pipes, they're ready to go up again. All but one of them are in place and the last one is ready to be fitted. Careful there! Easy, now! Watch out! Catch it! CRASH!

The boys come in from the drill field at 4:30 and head for the showers. There is no hot water.

"Get a load of that Hargrove," they fume, in an unnecessarily nasty manner. "He gets a job where all he has to do is to throw a shovel of coal on the fire every two hours. And then when we come in, there ain't no hot water. There ain't even no fire. Throw the bum out."

"Hargrove," the sergeant says quietly, "put down that rifle. It isn't loaded."

16. I GRINNED WEAKLY as I reported to the supply sergeant for work. "You must be that nice Sergeant Thomas W. Israel I've heard so many nice things about."

"No, little man," he said. "I'm the nice Sergeant Israel you've been running your loud mouth about. I'm the nice sergeant who always gives you the wrong clothing sizes and hides your laundry and does all those awful things you've been telling about me."

"So help me, sergeant," I protested. "I never named thee but to praise. Somebody's been trying to poison your mind against me. I didn't say any one of those nasty things. It was Grinny Miller."

"I am also the nice sergeant," he said, "who is going to let you earn your seventy cents today. Take off your fatigue blouse, my man, and prepare to sweat. Today we make progress. We are going to unpack rifles."

It seems to me that when the manufacturer prepares to pack a box of Army rifles, his cruel streak comes out at its worst. From the look of the rifles, he has his three-year-old daughter prepare a compound of molasses, pitch, and used motor oil—the gooier the better. He slings each gun into the resulting mess, sloshes it around for a while, and then lays it neatly into the box. What happens to the yardbird who has to unpack and clean the guns shouldn't happen to my worst enemy.

You use a swab about the size of a tablecloth to wipe the grease from the rifle. When you're halfway through the first rifle, you have to use the gun to wipe the grease from the cloth. When you have finished, you need a large coal shovel to wipe the grease off yourself.

There is nothing so conducive to itching as the inability to scratch. Just when the molasses-pitch-axle grease mixture covers your hands to the point where you can't see the outlines of the fingers, that left nostril starts tingling. At first it itches only a little and you decide to suffer it. So you don't wipe your hands on the seat of your trousers. Instead you pick up another rifle and your hand sinks to the elbow in the goo which wraps it. That is the stage where your nose gets peevish and impatient and decides to itch in earnest.

Finally, you decide to give in. You wipe your hands—an operation which takes a good three or four minutes for satisfactory results. You lift your hand to scratch your nose, only to find that your nose isn't itching any more.

You shrug philosophically and go back to work. As soon as you pick up another rifle and get your hands hopelessly stickied, the whole routine starts all over again. You grit your teeth and determine not to worry about nose itches. The nose insists. Finally, after a Spartan struggle with your inner self, you slowly lay the rifle down, pounce at your nose with both hands—grease and all—and curse with unexpected vigor. The cursing makes you feel so much better that you continue to shout your billingsgate until the nice supply sergeant puts his head around the corner and heaves an old shoe at you.

I was doing fairly well this morning, even when you take the itch into consideration, until the mess sergeant happened to stroll by.

"Hello, little man," he sings gaily, with a horrible gleam in his eye. "You've not been around to see me for a long time. Aren't mad, are you?"

I look at my hands, at the rifle, at the old shoe, and at the mess sergeant. I hold my tongue. Health is wealth.

"We miss you terribly in the kitchen," he coos, "even when you go griping around that my food is the worst in the Army. I just saw the first sergeant and I asked him to let you be a KP just as soon as he can spare you.

Oh, we're going to do wonders to that kitchenware, you and I."

He pats me on the forehead with ominous tenderness and departs. Five paces away, he turns for a parting shot. "Blabbermouth!" he snorts.

I suppose he's good to his mother, though.

17. THE SERGEANT YELLED OUT THE WINDOW at me, so I dropped my broom in the battery street and went upstairs. He was sitting on the foot locker, thoughtfully rubbing his chin with the handle of his mess-kit knife.

"Ralph Oxford got called up to the battery commander's office this morning," he said, "and do you know what the Old Man gave him?"

"I've got a pretty good idea," I said. "If he gave him what he gave me when I got called up, it has four letters, starts with an *h* and ends with an *l*."

The sergeant closed his eyes and slowly shook his head. "Oxford isn't a sore thumb to the platoon like you are," he groaned. "Oxford got a bright red stripe to wear around his sleeve."

"Oxford's no fireman," I told him.

"You're dern right he ain't," said the sergeant. "Starting with today, Oxford and Zuber and Roff and Macie-

jewski and Pappas and Mihalakakos are acting
corporals!"

I knew there must be a moral to all this, so I waited
for him to go on.

"Now, why couldn't you have been one of those six
boys?" he asked.

"Me?" The idea had never occurred to me. "I'm just
not the executive type, I suppose. Back at the *News,* the
boss told me that if I stayed there sixty years, I'd never
get promoted. I'm just not the type that gets promoted."

"Let's look at the record," said the sergeant. He
pulled his little black notebook from his pocket.

"On the drill field Saturday morning, you pulled
forty-eight boners out of fifty marching commands.
Everything you did was backwards.

"Friday morning you fell out for reveille without
your leggins. Saturday you had your leggins but no
field hat. Monday morning neither of your shoes was
tied and none of your shirt buttons were buttoned.
Tuesday morning it was without leggins again."

"I'm never really awake," I protested, "until ten
o'clock."

"You ain't awake then," he scoffed. "Every Monday
morning without fail I have to wake you up at least a
dozen times. I have to look behind all the posts around
here to see which one you're sleeping against. You snore
and disturb your classes, too!"

He was exaggerating there, I told him, I don't snore.

46

And I'm sleepy only on Monday morning. The rest of the time I'm alert and energetic.

"You're too energetic sometimes!" he roared. "Just this morning, when the lieutenant was coaching the platoon in rifle sighting and you were on fatigue duty as usual! That was a pretty one! You ran up and down the battery street twenty-two times in thirty minutes and you saluted the lieutenant every time you passed him! Do you think he ain't got a thing to do but return your salutes all morning?"

This was evidently a rhetorical question, so I didn't answer it.

"You don't salute an officer every time you see him when you're right there at his side practically all day. You salute him the first time you see him and the last time you're going to see him.

"And then when the lieutenant explains that to you," he sighed, "then what do you do! The next time you see him, you salute him again and then ask him was you supposed to salute him that time!"

He put his head in his hands and drummed sadly on the toe of his foot locker. He raised his head after a time and looked into the notebook again.

I knew what was coming next and I edged toward the door.

"And then you low-rated the mess sergeant's recipe for creamed beef on toast and told him his chow was the worst in the Army. And you said you was going to start eating in the next battery. That hurt his feelings

47

so bad that he burned the potatoes for the next three meals!"

I promised to apologize to the mess sergeant. The sergeant read out of his notebook for five or six minutes more, enumerating the things I had consistently done wrong.

"Now do you know," he asked wearily, "why you don't get the red stripes when they give them out?"

"I suppose I'm just not the executive type," I told him.

18. A MESS SERGEANT, ACCORDING TO MILI-TARY LEGEND, is a cook whose brains have been baked out. This does not apply to the mess sergeant in our battery, whose feelings are easily hurt by cruel remarks and who weeps tears into the mashed potatoes when he's picked on. This is simply the old Army definition of a mess sergeant.

All of us rising student cooks are eligible to become mess sergeants, Staff Sergeant Adams told us in our first cooking class yesterday morning. Then we can sit out in the cool dining rooms and yell back orders for the cooks to yell at the student cooks to yell at the kaypees.

This is not the beautiful goldbricking life that it

seems, though. The mess sergeant has to make requisitions and keep records on all the rations, he has to make out the menus, see that the food is prepared properly and supervise the work of the cooks, the student cooks, and the kaypees. Besides this, he must listen to all the gripes about his food and to the threadbare jokes about cooks who get drunk from lemon and vanilla extract.

All this he must do, with his brains baked out.

The cook, lucky little rascal that he is, also leads an ideal life. He is allowed to believe that he knows more about cooking than the mess sergeant will ever know, although he is not supposed to tell the mess sergeant that he does. He works one day and sleeps the next two.

If the cook is not feeling cheerful, he can pick on at least one student cook and at least five kaypees. On the battlefield, he is in the safest position behind the lines, since the food is endowed with more sentimental value than the top sergeant. The jokes about Army cooks' being shot at from both sides are not based upon fact.

However, friend cook has to greet the morn before the morn gets there. On the days when he works, he has to get up between 3:00 and 3:30 o'clock in order to prepare a substantial breakfast for about two hundred healthy, growing boys whose appetites are exceeded only by the size of their mouths and the power of their lungs.

Yesterday we started to school, with cookbooks and manuals and loose-leaf notebooks for our homework. The only way in which it differed from public schools was that the naughty boys didn't have to go and sit with the girls. Also, the dunce seat, instead of being in the corner of the classroom, was said to be behind a large sack of potatoes in the battery kitchen.

The only hope for an easy time in class was gone in this school. There's no percentage in bringing a shiny red apple to a teacher who has the key to at least one well-stocked pantry.

Tomorrow, after lunch, each of us will be taken to one of the sixty-four Replacement Center kitchens. There we will present ourselves to the mess sergeant, who will sigh wearily at the sight of us and show us where to change our uniforms. Then we will proceed to prove, in our respective kitchens, the old saw about too many cooks.

We will be railed at by the mess sergeant and the first cook and, if we want to and know how to, we can rail at the kaypees in turn. When the boys in line make sneering remarks about having spinach again already, we can jaw back at them. It will be wonderful to be able to jaw at someone again. Life has loveliness to sell.

19. IN THE KITCHEN, THEY TELL US, all the cleaning-up work is to be done by the kaypees, so that the cook may be doing more important things. This, unfortunately, doesn't apply to the daily task of cleaning the stoves thoroughly. The stoves, it says here in the books, are the cook's tools and he must do his own grinding.

It isn't worth the time to wait for the stoves to get comfortably cool before you begin the twilight beautification of these overgrown infernos. In order to avoid the rush at the theater, and to let the kaypees off early, start work now.

The stoves must be cleaned inside and out—thoroughly. First, shake down the fire. All the live coals must go into the ashpan under the grate. That much is simple. Then remove the ashpan, red coals and all. It must be dumped into the ash can out on the garbage rack. This entire procedure should be simple, too, it says here. All you have to do is to catch the front handle with a heavy glove and catch the little hook in the rear with the far end of your cap lifter. Here we go!

Carry the ashpan well in front of you. Ain't it hot! When you get to the door, simply open it with the toe of your shoe. Like this. Like— Doesn't seem to work. Try again. Try pushing the right screen so that the left one will swing slightly toward you. Ready? Slightly push the right screen. Something seems to be wrong here.

During this time, you will become increasingly aware that the glove over the ashpan handle is becoming hotter and hotter. Just as you get your toe into the door, the heat penetrates the glove and you decide— very suddenly—that perhaps it's best to drop the whole matter. Drop it slowly, carefully, tenderly—if you can.

Do not drop it upon the wooden floor. Look around, if you think you have time, and locate an overturned boiler on which to set it. Whew, that hand's hot! No boiler? Then drop it anyway!

You will find that dropping the ashpan, even though you did it gently, has released a small amount of floating ash, all of which will be absorbed into your mouth and nose. Patience, brother. See that the ashpan isn't lying where it will burn anything, such as a perfectly good wooden floor. Pour cold water on the glove, wait for the resulting steam to blow away, prop open the door as you should have done in the first place, and try, try again.

This time you will almost reach the garbage rack before the glove again gets hot. Slide, Kelly, slide! You won't get there without dropping the whole pan into the clean road, but at least you tried.

Beat the pan against the ash can several times for sound effect. Return to the kitchen, where the mess sergeant, who was watching you through the window all the time, will direct you to return and clean it up.

When this job is completed, take hope and courage. You have only two more ashpans to empty.

Then you may get to work cleaning out all the soot which has gathered above and below the ovens. In this procedure, a small, solid-surface rake is inserted through a tiny door in front. Using the door as a base of operations, wiggle that pesky little thing around inside the long, wide, low space, pulling out load after load of soot. The work will teach you muscular co-ordination, manual dexterity, the art of contortion, humility and, several dozen new cuss words you didn't even know you knew.

Rake, rake, rake. Time marches on. Still more raking. Like the magic pitcher in the old Greek legend, the more you take out the more there is inside. The soot from all three oven jackets will fill one large ashpan, at a double-tablespoonful the rake.

By the time you have finished and look about you, the kaypees have finished their work and are sitting around gaping at you as if you were a steam shovel. A very, very black steam shovel.

Isn't gas a wonderful fuel?

20. PRIVATE SHER AND I WERE SITTING out on the back steps to dodge the cleaning work going on inside when we saw the sergeant bearing down on us from the other end of the battery street.

"It's no use scooting inside, Hargrove," said Sher. "He's already seen us. Look tired, as if you'd already done your part of the work." Private Sher is the gold-bricking champion of Battery A and always knows what to do in such an emergency.

We both draped expressions of fatigue over our faces and the sergeant skidded to a halt before us. He reached into his hip pocket for the little black book and aimed a finger at both of us.

"Bums!" he shouted. "Bums! I worked my fingers to the bone yesterday morning getting this platoon to pretty up the barracks for inspection. Comes inspection and two privates have dirty shoes lying sprawled all over the floor under their bunks! Private Hargrove and MISTER Private Sher! Report to Corporal Farmer in fatigue clothes."

We reported to Corporal Farmer, who looked at his list of jobs. "As much as you don't deserve it," he said, "you two goldbricks are in line for canteen police."

Mr. Private Sher and I walked up the battery street toward the canteen.

"Is this canteen police business good or bad?" I asked.

"Oh, so-so," he said. "You have to clean up the papers and cigarette butts around the post exchange first thing in the morning. Then you come around and check up three or four times during the day."

I stopped, aghast. "What do you do betweentimes?"

"Just be inconspicuous," said Sher. "That's all there is to it. Please pick up that candy wrapper over there. My back aches."

We cleaned up the grounds around the post exchange and sat for a while in the shade, watching a battery going through calisthenics. With beautiful precision, the soldiers swung their rifles up, down, to the right, to the left. They went through the quarter, half, and full knee bends and the shoulder exercises and the rest of the routine.

"Those boys seem to be improving, Mr. Sher," I said.

"Result of hard work," said Maury. "Personally, I get awfully tired watching this. We'll wear ourselves out. Let's go over to my kitchen and handshake for a bottle of milk."

"No," I protested. "We must go to my kitchen."

"To avoid a tiring argument," suggested Private Sher, "we will go to both our kitchens. We can't be thrown out of both of them."

After successful forays on both kitchens, Private Sher began to yawn with boredom. "My dear Hargrove," he said, "we must stimulate our minds. Let us adjourn to my place for a game of checkers." Private Sher's "place" was only one flight of stairs removed from my squad-room, so we adjourned.

After two games of checkers, Private Sher waved his arms. "This is folderol," he said. "You are no checker player, Hargrove. You have no idea of tactics. Let us sit by the window and watch our comrades drill. There is something stirring in the sight of fine young men perfectly executing a marching order."

While we were sitting there being stirred, another corporal disturbed us. He wanted us to go with him to haul coal.

"Much as we would like to help you haul coal, my good man," said Maury, "we are now actively engaged in the work of policing up the post exchange. Feel free to call upon us at any other time."

The corporal placed his hands on his hips and stared

at us. "You're being punished," he asked, "with canteen duty?"

"There's no need to be vulgar," said Sher. "If you will excuse us, it is time for us to go again to look for cigarette butts around the post exchange. Coming, Mr. Hargrove?"

"Coming, Mr. Sher. And a good day to you, corporal!"

21. WHEN JUNIOR COMES HOME FROM CAMP on furlough or for the weekend, he probably will throw out his chest, pull his shoulders almost out of joint, and speak a sort of jargon entirely unintelligible to you. There is no cause for alarm; Junior is merely exaggerating to show off his familiarity with military life.

You will not be consoled by this knowledge when he begins speaking this unknown tongue. In order to understand some of his conversation, you might tear out this page and tuck it away in the drawer with your recipes and patterns.

Goldbricking is an Army term signifying, in a word, loafing. In its strictest sense, it means avoiding your fair share of the work, thus making the load harder for the other boys. When Junior uses the term, however, it merely means hiding from the work in the first place or stretching an easy job out to make it last as long as possible.

Batting the breeze is the military equivalent of "bull-shooting."

Police, as nearly as it can be explained, means "to clean up" or "to keep clean." Examples are kitchen police, or kaypee, canteen police, and police the area.

Fatigue duty is work that is not actual military training, but a part of the turnabout method of getting the dirty work done. Fatigue clothes are the blue denims worn for extra duty. Regular uniforms are called OD's, an abbreviation for "olive drab."

GI is short for "Government Issue." GI soap is the yellow laundry soap, a GI brush is a hard-bristle scrub-bing brush, and a GI haircut is the regulation style which sacrifices two-thirds of Junior's wavy locks to cleanliness and sanitation.

The *PX* is the post exchange, or canteen, a co-opera-tive enterprise which sells practically everything the soldier needs. Three times a month, canteen books of credit tickets may be obtained in denominations from one to five dollars. Ten per cent of the proceeds from these are returned to the battery fund, which is used to buy nonessentials for the battery.

The *old man* is the battery commander, who may also be referred to among yourselves as the BC or the skipper. The top kick is a first sergeant, the chief of the battery's noncommissioned officers.

Jawbone is an apt word meaning "credit." A jawbone

corporal is an acting corporal, who has neither the rating nor the pay of a corporal.

A *guardhouse lawyer* is a self-appointed legal expert who knows all there is to know about the laws and rights of soldiers, he says. The Congressional legislation for military discipline is contained in "the book," a manual of court-martial known as the Articles of War. The 96th Article of War, which you've heard about, is the one which provides punishment for "conduct unbecoming to a soldier." When you are sentenced for a number of violations simultaneously, they "throw the book at you."

Over the hill is an artistic way of referring to unauthorized absence. This is another expression for AWOL.

Food is *chow* or *mess*. Stew is slum or slum-gullion. Salt pork, which you rarely see in the Army, is called lamb chop. "They lam it against the wall to get the salt out of it and then they chop it up into the beans."

To *fall out,* soldiers vacate the barracks quickly, before the sergeant gets really mad. To fall in, they take their places in ranks.

A *yardbird* is the lowest form of animal life in an Army camp. Under the common law, he is rated as one rank below a buck private. The yardbird, for this misdeed or that shortcoming, spends most of his time in menial labor about the battery area.

When Junior refers to a yardbird, you will notice, he is invariably speaking of someone else.

22. IT WAS OUR AFTERNOON OFF and we were lying around in our barracks, too lazy to dress for a movie or a trip to the Service Club. All of us were, that is, except Private Zuber. With an enthusiasm and energy foreign to a cook's afternoon off, Zuber was applying a blinding glaze to his shoes. This finished, he connected an iron and began sharpening the creases in his trousers.

"Going somewhere, I take it," asked Private Clarkin, the Jersey milkman.

Private Zuber grinned happily, and nodded. He donned his fresh clothing, gave his necktie several unnecessary tugs, and combed his hair for the twelfth time.

Private McGlauflin, late of the Minneapolis bar, laid down his copy of the *Bartender's Guide* and sat up on his bunk. "Didn't you know?" he asked. "Zuber's girl's come down from Rochester. They're going riding."

"That's a fine thing," crowed Clarkin. "I haven't been for a spin since I've been here. Get your shoes on, Hargrove. And straighten your name plate, McGlauflin. We must make a good impression on our guest. . . ."

"You sure are a pleasant surprise, ma'am," Clarkin prattled on to the pretty girl in the front seat. "Fancy Ben Zuber even knowing anybody like you. You should see the homely looking things he brings to the dances here."

She smiled a polite thank-you at Clarkin and glanced sharply at Zuber. "I never could even get him to the dances at home," she said. "He wouldn't even look at the girls at all. Would you, dear?"

"No, ma'am," groaned the martyred Zuber, who spent almost all his evening hours writing letters to Rochester.

"Just to look at Ben," said McGlauflin, "you'd never think such a quiet-seeming boy could raise so much devil. It constantly amazes me."

Private Zuber's girl friend's smile was not so spontaneous this time, and there was a baleful gleam in her glance at poor Benjamin. "What have you been doing, dear?" she asked with terrible gentleness.

Private McGlauflin went on glibly. "Tell her about the time you got tight in Fayetteville and tried to take the policeman's hat away from him, Ben!"

The one-girl audience was shocked. Her expression, as she looked at Zuber, was one of anxiety and doubt.

Clarkin began again. "And the terrible fight he had that time—ooof!" McGlauflin gave him a hearty dig in the ribs. To make sure that it had registered and created sufficient horrible curiosity in the feminine mind, he repeated it.

Private Zuber, guiltless but helpless, drooped his shoulders further as the terrible ride continued. "Here's the Service Club, dear," he finally said. "Shall we go in and have something to drink?" He gave the three of us a pathetically beseeching glance.

"They don't sell lemon extract in there, Zuber," I suggested. Clarkin, McGlauflin, and I exchanged looks that purposed to show a hidden knowledge of another terrible paragraph in the collapse of the soul of Benjamin Zuber.

We sat at a table in the Service Club drinking the sodas our victim bought for us. Clarkin looked long at his glass of water.

"The sight of water," he remarked, "reminds me of what the sergeant was telling Ben last week about daily bathing."

McGlauflin took pity on the innocent Zuber, who was dying for a cause he knew not. "We'll have to be going. We have things to do and I imagine you two young people want to enjoy each other's company."

"Yes," said Zuber's fiancée slowly. "Ben and I have SO much to talk about." Private Zuber shuddered and his shoulders slumped tragically.

"We certainly have enjoyed the afternoon," crowed Clarkin. "Lovely time."

The three of us—Clarkin, McGlauflin, and I—went whistling down the street, little caring what the morrow might bring. To finish the afternoon, we short-sheeted five bunks in the next barracks.

23. ONE OF THE FIRST PEOPLE I LOOKED UP
when I went to Charlotte on leave was Ward Beecher
Threatt, who writes a column of sorts for the Saturday
edition of the Charlotte *News.*

"Well, Hargrove," began the postcard philosopher,
"how's the Army agreeing with you? I've been aching
to find out what you've been doing." This was a subtle
slam at my column.

"Well, all things considered—" I began.

"Nothing like the Army," said Ward Beecher. "I
wouldn't take a million dollars for the time I spent in
it. Nobody'd offer me a million anyway. Have you got
a rating yet?"

"Well—" I began again.

"Lord, did I have my ups and downs! Got all the
way up to sergeant three times and was busted three
times—for the good of the service." He paused to light
another cigarette and I thought I saw an opening.

"Let me tell you about the trip over," I said. "We
left the—"

"We started a crap game on the train," said Threatt,
"and I had to wire home for money before I got to
Rock Hill. Have you had a payday yet?"

"We'll have one—" I started.

"On that ocean voyage," he broke in, "I went for
fourteen days without a cigarette. I followed one man
all around the boat waiting for him to throw away a

62

butt. Instead of throwing it on the deck, where I could have scooped it, he flung it over the rail. I followed another and just when I thought he'd be ready to throw it away, I asked him for the butt. The son-of-a-gun told me he had three different kinds of colds—and he threw his cigarette over the side. He didn't have another, he said."

"Did I tell you about our first day at Fort Bragg?" I asked him.

"We landed at Brest," he said, "and we had to walk up one of the longest derned hills I've ever seen before we could drop our suitcases. The Frenchmen swarmed around us, selling everything from steamer trunks to fine-toothed combs. Twenty of us boys pooled our pocket money to buy a pack of cigarettes for fifty cents. What are you going to spend your first pay on?"

"Oh, I suppose I'll—"

"First payday I had I went out and bought myself a pack of cigarettes and lay awake almost all night smoking them. Best cigarettes I ever tasted. By the way, how's the food at Fort Bragg?"

"I find it very—"

"Over in France we used to take our drinking water and swap it to the French for wine. It was a tossup which tasted worse—our water or their wine. Ah, them was the days! Like your uniform?"

"I think it's very—"

"Nothing like the ones we wore. There we were, in the hottest part of the summer, with these woolen OD's,

Russian high collars, wrap-around leggins, and all the works. How do you like my costume?"

"Well, confidentially—"

"This field cap ain't the one they issued to me. I lost that one and had to help myself to this one. I wouldn't tell you where I got it. I used to get into more potato-peeling work for not getting this collar fixed right, too. Looks right distinguished, doesn't it?"

I looked at the modernistic clock on Ward Beecher's parlor table. I took my eyes off it quickly, lest he tell me again about how he won it at the fireman's convention.

"Well, Ward," I said, jumping desperately into a gap in the conversation, "I've enjoyed talking to you about my life in the Army, but I have to get along uptown again. I've got—"

"Sure thing, fellow," said the man of letters; "it certainly is interesting to hear from a soldier in this army. I could listen to you for hours."

"Hey, Hargrove," he yelled as I started up the street "next time you come, remind me to tell you about my job as a pilot in the old war!"

24. WHEN A SERGEANT TELLS YOU that it's the little things in life that are important, he's not just saying it. A sergeant who impresses that one corny slice of homely philosophy upon a rookie's mind is giving him one of the most important lessons of his Army life.

The soldier has a thousand and one small things to remember in his everyday life. Most of these he forgets at least once before a noncom etches them vividly on his mind with kitchen duty.

One of these small things is the identification disk, or "dog tag," of which each man wears a pair. Dog tags are supposed to be worn at all times. A soldier will wear his tag all through the day, taking it off only for a shower. After he takes his shower, he probably will forget to put the tag back on—at least, if he has a memory like mine. He never misses it until the next morning when he's taking calisthenics. Then he doesn't know that he doesn't have it until he sees the sergeant come over to him, look for the tag and write his name down in the little black book.

At retreat, the afternoon inspection of the soldiers, I always check everything before I fall out for the once-over. Are my shoes shined? Is my rifle cleaned and oiled? Does my belt buckle shine? Is my name plate pinned straight over my left shirt pocket? Can I get by with this morning's shave? Do I need a haircut? Are all my pockets buttoned? When I make sure that everything is as it should be, I sigh with satisfaction and fall out.

The battery assembles in a neat, precise picture of mass formation. The battery commander orders the top kick to "Prepare the battery for inspection!" The top kick opens the ranks and the lines straighten out to perfection. From where I stand, everything looks perfect.

The battery commander begins his inspection. Until he gets almost to me, I feel almost smug to think that for once I've stood retreat and not fallen short somewhere. To bask in my own perfection, I sneak a forbidden peek at my gun and uniform.

Then, to my horror, I see two shiny strands of stainless steel just below my belt—the chain on that dadblasted dollar watch! Your whole day can be spoiled by doodads such as that marring the neatness and simplicity of your uniform. Back to the kitchens, Dulcy!

There's one good thing, however, about forgetting to take off your nonkosher watch chain for retreat, or to put on your leggins for reveille, or to straighten the shoes under your bunk. After the first time, you remember them!

POSTAL NOTE: In cooking class yesterday, we were issued report cards to be delivered to the mess sergeants in the kitchens where we are apprentices. According to straight dope from the orderly room, those of us who fail miserably in military and culinary instruction, or who show uncalled-for popularity in the little black books, during the three-month training will be called upon to repeat the course. Unless the new leaf turns me over, my address will be Battery A for the "Duration."

VOCABULARY LESSON: A new rank among the non-commissioned officers, announces the grapevine comic page, is the rank of metal sergeant. The rank is conferred only by the men in the ranks, and a metal sergeant is distinguished by "the silver in his hair, the gold in his teeth, and the lead in his pants." In order to avoid strained relations at Fort Bragg, let it be understood that there are no metal sergeants in Battery A.

Whew, that could have been a close one!

25. THE NEW STUDENT COOK laid down his meat knife, wiped his hands on his apron, and leaned against the serving counter.

"Reminds me," he said, "of a friend of mine, used to live in New York."

We had already learned to listen when the new student cook professed to be "reminded" of something. The work was slack, so we lighted up cigarettes and got comfortable.

"Seems this friend of mine—name was Harvey Helding—lost his job in New York and he'd been staying at this boardinghouse and hadn't paid his board for about five weeks. Didn't feel any too good about getting that far behind with his board, but the landlady and her husband were real nice about it, so he stayed.

"Finally, one day, this friend of mine decided to make one more stab at finding a job, and if he didn't find one he was aiming to come back to Florida. Well, he was down to his last quarter, so the landlady fixed him a lunch to take with him."

The new student cook paused, contemplated his fingernails, and went on:

"Well, he took a bus uptown. Wasn't but one empty seat on the bus and that was right next to a nice, sweet-looking old lady. He wasn't going to sit down beside her, but she looked up over at him and saw him standing up. 'Young man,' she says, 'you can come over and sit by me.' So Harvey did. She talked to him for a while and she seemed to be a real nice old lady.

"Well, the conductor came around to take up the tickets and this friend of mine gave him a token he had besides his last quarter. So when the conductor asked the old lady for her ticket, she said she didn't have one. Well, Harvey didn't want to see a scene made, so he paid her fare. Well, instead of thanking him, the old lady wanted the twenty cents change he got back. Kept after him for it until he gave it to her."

The new cook stopped for a minute and looked intently at the stoves. We wondered if his story had finished. Finally he resumed it.

"Well, when this friend of mine got up to get off the bus at his stop, he saw that the old lady had left a fancy-wrapped package like a gift or something behind her when she had got up. He took the package.

"Forgot all about it being in his coat pocket until the end of the day. Well, he hadn't done a bit of good all day towards finding work, but when he came back to his boardinghouse, he gave the package to his landlady as a present.

"Well, the next morning when he went down to tell the landlady he was going to have to move out, she met him at the stairs and threw her arms around his neck and kissed him. 'Mr. Helding,' she said to him, 'you're the most thoughtful person ever! That was exactly what I had been wanting for a long time! I think you're just a darling!' And she proceeded to make over him all during breakfast.

"Soon as breakfast was over, the landlady's husband took this friend of mine aside and told him, he said, 'Now lookahere, Mr. Helding, you and me have been friends for a long time. I feel just like you were my son. That's why I'm not going to get nasty about this. I'm just going to ask you—don't you ever give my wife any more gifts like that!'

"Well, this friend of mine didn't know what to make of it all, so he went to the landlady and he told her, said he was awful sorry, but he just hadn't been able to find work yet and he didn't have any more money, so he was just going to have to leave. The landlady, she came over and patted his shoulder and said, 'Mr. Helding, your board is paid up for as long as you want to stay here. I couldn't think of turning out anybody who'd given me such a thoughtful present as you gave me yesterday, when you probably spent your last penny on it. You just stay on here and you'll find a job. But if you ever want to give me another present, get me another box of the same.' So he stayed on and found a job in less than two weeks."

"So come on," one of the kaypees asked, "what was in the package?"

"I haven't the slightest idea," said the new student cook.

26. ONE OF THE NICEST THINGS about working in the kitchen in Battery C of the 13th Battalion has been the knowledge that its number-one chow hound, Buster Charnley, would drop around after supper and chew the conversational fat. It's like a letter from home to listen to Buster's slow and mournful drawl, and his refreshingly dry humor is a pick-me-up at the end of a long, hot afternoon.

Buster came prancing up the chow line the other evening with a grin that started at the back of his head and enveloped his face from the nose down.

"What's eating you, Walter," I asked him, "—besides that egg-sucking grin?"

"Leaving here, boy!" he sang. "You won't see me

around for three months. And when you see me, son, you'll see stripes on my sleeves and a look of prosperity on my clean-cut Tarheel face!"

The man behind him wanted to get to the mashed potatoes, so Buster had to move on down the line. I got the whole story from one of the kaypees while I waited for him to make his evening call.

Of the 200-odd men in Battery C, two men had been selected for three months' training at Fort Sill, Oklahoma. At the end of their three months, they will come back as gunnery instructors, with a noncommissioned officer's rating and a specialist's extra pay on top of that. Mrs. Walter Charnley's little boy Buster was one of the two men selected.

I was chopping kindling for breakfast when Buster came around again, and I painted Fort Sill as a nest of jack rabbits, gophers, and rattlesnakes and assured him that Battery C was sending him to school to cut down the grocery bills. If we hadn't been insulting each other in a friendly fashion for years, I would have told him that I wasn't particularly astonished and that I was sure he'd make a good instructor and the kind of noncommissioned officer the boys borrow money from.

Battery C will miss Ole Buster while he's away. The cooks will miss him because he always remembers to compliment them when he likes the meat loaf or the cherry cobbler. The mess sergeant will miss him because he livens the kitchen when it comes his turn to do kaypee. The boys will miss him because he's one of the best-liked boys there.

One of the sergeants near here came back from a recent leave with one of the most glorious shiners that ever darkled the human eye.

"Run into a door?" I asked him.

"Gave a guy the wrong answer," he replied simply, "or, rather, the answer he didn't want."

I looked at his face; his teeth were all there and his jaw was still in one piece. I looked at his hands; the knuckles showed the marks of service.

"I was at a party," he went on, "when this fellow who lives next door to my folks wants to know 'how's the morale in the Army?' 'Excellent,' I tell him; 'excellent!' He looks me up and down sort of pitying-like and wants to know don't I read the magazine stories about how poor it is. Well, I tell him, 'I spend all my time with the boys and I believe what I see more than what I read.'

"He goes on from there making cracks at the Army and the country and the suckers we are for giving our time for what's not worth fighting for in the first place. I listen politely for a while, because even though I'm not in uniform I don't want to look rowdy. I stand as much as I can and then I ask him to his feet. It isn't long before his three brothers join the fight. It was one of the brothers put his finger ring in my eye."

"Brother," I told him, "that ain't a black eye. That's a badge."

"I lost the fight," he said.

"You won the argument, though," I told him.

I'd like to use the sergeant's name, but he made me promise not to.

"I told the Old Man," he said, "that I got the shiner playing baseball."

27. "HOW CAN I FIT YOU INTO A COAT," moaned Supply Sergeant Israel, "with you fidgeting around like a race horse at the post? Stand still, dern you, stand still!"

"Heavens to Betsy, Thomas," I complained, "you're getting to be the fussiest old maid in the outfit. I'm not squirming!"

"In the first place, my man," he said, "don't call me Thomas or try to get overly familiar with your elders and betters. In the second place, don't argue with me. In the third place, don't fidget in the first place. And in the fourth place, don't agitate me unnecessarily. I'm at the end of my patience with you and I ain't feeling in no holiday spirit anyway."

I buttoned the handsome winter blouse and he stepped back to inspect it with the eye of an artist. "Every time my wife gets mad at me, she has her picture taken to send to me. The picture I got today showed she's going to eat my heart out unmercifully when I can't put off my furlough any longer and I have to go home. And with domestic difficulties on my hands, I have to fit your winter uniforms."

He yanked at my coattail, straightened the collar and scratched his head. "Hargrove—37 long," he yelled to the boy at the desk.

"Man that is born of woman," I comforted him, "is of many days and full of trouble."

"Git off the platform and into this overcoat," he sighed. He held the coat while I got into it and he slapped my hand for fidgeting again. "Sometimes I wonder why I go to so much trouble keeping you boys dressed right. Here I spend the whole afternoon wiping sweat out of my eyebrows, just to see that your clothes fit you and you won't look like a bunch of bums—which you are.

"Do you know what some ungrateful kitchen termite said the other day? He started putting it around that the Army could double itself in half an hour by filling up the extra space in its trousers. Do your trousers fit you, bum?" He straightened the pleats in the back of the overcoat and gave the tail an unnecessarily vicious yank.

"Did I say they didn't?" I groaned, raising my arms despairingly. "Just because somebody else says you stretch the coat in the back so the man will think it fits right in front, you have to go picking on me!"

"Me pick on you?" he screamed. "It's a wonder my nerves ain't completely shot! Do I come around and put signs on *your* door saying, 'Walk Up One Flight and Save Five Dollars'? Do I throw gunny sacks on *your* bed and ask you to take up the cuffs two inches?

"With my thankless job, it's a wonder I haven't collapsed before this. I wish I was a permanent kitchen police instead of a supply sergeant. Hargrove—37 long! NEXT!"

MEN'S FASHIONS: Beginning October 1, the well-dressed man in the $21 income bracket will discard khaki two-piece suits with matching cravats for well-cut woolens, with black as the predominant color in neckties. The use of brass buttons will be popular. Underthings will be longer than the summer scanties, although not so long as the provincially perennial woolie-woolies. Little change will be seen in shoe styles. Olive drab is definitely predicted as the color sensation of the season.

HAVE A CHESTNUT: They're telling the story now about the draftee who kept going around the camp picking up pieces of paper. He'd examine them, say, "That's not it," and walk on, mumbling to himself. After several days of this, an officer decided the boy was crazy, so he took him to the doctor. The doctor kept him under observation and after several days of that "That's not it" business, agreed with the officer. When he wrote out a discharge slip and handed it to the officer, the selectee pounced upon it and sighed. "That's it!" he said.

28. "THIS BATTERY IS MY BABY," Corporal
Henry Ussery said, loosening his belt for a real bull
session. "I've watched it grow from thutty-one men to
what it is now. It was hard work building up this battery to what it is now, but it's worth it when you look
around and see what you've done."

The assembly sighed en masse and decided to loosen
its belts. Ussery was wound up again.

"When I got here, there wasn't anybody here but the
instructors. We spent four weeks eating dust and running rabbits. There I was—I'd spent thutteen months
learning the old drill and tactics to where I reckon I
had it down better than any man in the whole Army.
Then they started this 'minute Army,' with a bunch
of green, ignorant Yankees—and I had to teach them
what they had to know!"

The bull session nodded wisely and Corporal Ussery
went on. "Now, this young Corporal Joe Gantt, for
instance. Now, this Corporal Gantt, when he first came
in, was one of the greenest rookies in the bunch. But
he snapped out of it and made corporal in four
months."

"Was that soldiering," a voice broke in, "or handshaking—as the Latins used to say, *mittus floppus?*"

"Much as I can't stand Gantt, I'll have to admit it
was soldiering. That's the way it is. You sweat your
head off hammering the drills and the calisthenics and

the military courtesy and guard duty and the physical hygiene and the manual of arms into them. They're all clumsy and awkward as a bear in an egg crate at first, but then you can see them, after a while, snapping into it and getting better and better. By the time we've had them thutteen weeks, and they're ready to be assigned to their posts, they're as keen and alert as a bunch of West Point cadets. They're extra good cooks and better soldiers."

"Isn't a good soldier a specialist at griping and growling?" somebody asked him.

"When a soldier can gripe," the corporal announced in a pontifical manner, "he's happy as a pig in the sunshine. When he doesn't gripe, there's something wrong with him. That's another thing you learn. When you first came here, you didn't know the first principles of griping. You griped about the clothes; you griped about the beds; you griped especially about having to go to bed at nine o'clock.

"Griping is an art, just like goldbricking is an art. Before you leave here, you learn that you don't enjoy griping a bit when you spread your energy all over everywhere, griping about everything. You learn to choose one thing and specialize in griping about that.

"If you want to be a specialist at griping, you have to get on your toes. You get to where your clothes are comfortable. Where you used to think the food was terrible, now you pretend that you don't get enough of it. You like the beds and by nine o'clock you're sleepy. So you have to find something special to gripe about. If you haven't got any originality at all, pick you out one special noncom and gripe about him.

"Now, you take Private Hargrove, for instance. First came here, he griped about me telling him he was carrying his rifle wrong. Now he gripes when I tell him he's carrying it right. He might have something there. He still carries it like it was a 75-millimeter gun. He's getting so shiftless, even at griping, that he can't find anything to beef about except not getting any mail. I'm going to write all his creditors, so he won't even be able to gripe about the mail."

"That reminds me," I said. "Did I tell you boys what Sergeant Taylor told me about Ussery today?"

"Nine o'clock!" Ussery shouted. "Lights out! Break it up!"

29. SOMEWHERE ON THE WILD COAST of South Carolina, the battalion in which I cook is being treated to a weekend to combine business with pleasure. We can romp in the Atlantic while we get a "taste of the field." With the wind blowing the sand into kitchens and pup tents alike, it will be nice to get back to Fort Bragg for a taste of the food we eat. A vexed soldier here doesn't grate his teeth. He crunches them.

We made the trip here in lorries, which are the

mechanical age's nearest approach in appearance to covered wagons. You've probably seen them rolling noisily but smoothly through town—large canvas-topped trucks with a folding bench down each side inside. You'd expect to be hauled out of one of them, beaten to death, at the end of a 130-mile trip. They give a tolerably bumpy ride, just tolerably.

When we started pitching camp, about a quarter of a mile back from the beach, we found the place already inhabited—by cannibals. These creatures, which masquerade as harmless flies and even camouflaged by the harmless sounding name of sand flies, must have vampire blood back in the line somewhere.

I don't bear any grudge against the easygoing, good-natured house fly—in fact, I feel rather cruel when I squash one for tickling me—but it arouses my pioneer fighting spirit to see a stunted horsefly light on my bare leg, make himself sassily comfortable and start draining off my life's blood. But what can you do? Slapping one only serves to make him mad at you.

At night we sleep, or at least we simulate sleep, in pup tents, made by our own hands with loving care, blood, sweat, tears, two pieces of waterproof cloth, two lengths of rope, and a handful of turned lumber.

I share my little duplex with Private Warren, the new student cook who told me the story about the man at the boardinghouse. When I stumbled home last night, primed to the gills with a blend of sand and salt water, I discovered that we had an overnight guest! The chief cook on our shift, in the task of packing the field kitchen, had neglected to put his own field pack (tent half, blankets, etc.) on the truck, so he decided to drop over and have us put him up for the night.

A pup tent, as you probably don't need to be told, will accommodate two men, provided neither of them walks in his sleep. If three men are to sleep in one tent, at least two of them must be midgets or babes in arms. Cooks should never sleep two to a tent, because of their tendency toward plumpness.

We arranged ourselves in the tent by wrapping knees around the tent poles, putting all feet outside for the night and raising one side of the tent high enough to make a rustic sleeping porch of the whole affair.

The guest proved to be one of those loathsome creatures who pull all the cover to their side of the bed. We had quite a lot of trouble with him, since he slept in the middle and rolled up in both our blankets. We remedied this by waiting until he started snoring, then recovered our blankets, rolling ourselves in them and throwing a raincoat over him.

The three-man arrangement was very uncomfortable for a while, but when I woke the next morning I found that the night had been comfortable on the whole. When I finished opening my eyes by scooping the sand from them, I found that I had rolled out through the opened side of the tent and spent the night under a myrtle bush ten yards down the slope.

During my first off hour, I succeeded in getting a tan which must have darkened the very marrow of my bones. My chest, back, and legs looked the color of a faded danger flag and smelled like the roast pork that the cook forgot to watch. After that, the surf and the sun went their ways and I went mine.

My sole amusement now, when I can sneak away from the field kitchen, is in sitting on the porch of a drink stand, mooching ice cream from passing friends. The juke box inside has played incessantly since we first came here. Of the past 390 selections played, at least 389 have been "$21 a Day Once a Month." The boys all know the lyrics verbatim now and drown out the vocalist, which is some relief.

Whatta you say we go home now?

30. FOR ONCE I HAVE GONE ON SICK CALL for purposes other than goldbricking. This time it was for sympathy, tenderness, and sunburn lotion. I got the sunburn lotion. Since then I have been confined to quarters—a pathetic, lorn creature wandering about the squadroom in a minimum of clothing and a glow of brilliant red light.

Things are getting fairly comfortable for a while. The poet Droschniop and the happy warrior Menza applied the ointment with tender care. Private Sher was asked to snaffle a sandwich from the mess hall and returned with a laden tray, replete with iced tea and a double portion of dessert. By sitting on the floor on my heels, I was even able to start reading the novel that has been taking up space in my foot locker for weeks.

But night must fall. In a case like this, where you're packed in grease like a boxed rifle, it's best to place one layer of newspaper between sheet and blanket. After lying there for a while, listening to the news-papers crackle exactly like burnt flesh every time you twist in agony, you feel the urge to sit up and look at some real stars.

The next afternoon, shortly after lunch, I was perched on the edge of a table, feeling thankful that I had been able to get that far through the day without having to dress to go anywhere. I was just sitting there fanning myself with both hands, when Sergeant Schmidt came in.

"Hargrove, go to the orderly room. Telephone."

Since I knew quite well that no one was going to call me long distance—at day rates—for a casual conversa-tion, I hurriedly threw a raincoat over my lobster-colored frame, waited to regain my senses after the first sharp shock of pain, and dashed like a wild thing to the orderly room.

"Whatcha say thaah, boy?" a lazy voice drawled out of the receiver. "This is yo' ole frien', the Scarlet Ter-mite."

I was still half wild from the gouging of the oilskin into my back. "How're you, Termite?" I asked, not having the slightest idea who the Termite was.

"This is old True Blue, boy," the voice said. "I'm in Fayetteville now."

Much as I wanted to talk with old True Blue, I was in no condition.

"I'm selling insurance here now," True Blue went on.

"Don't want any," I said. "I can get it wholesale from the government." I looked nervously around to see if the battery commander was listening to this weird and unnecessary conversation going on over his telephone. Before I could get my neck completely turned, the gouging raincoat jerked me back. The friendly voice of True Blue went on and on, recalling incidents of our happy boyhood together. My skin began dancing under the coat and I knew how a medium well-done steak feels on the grill.

"I'll look you up, True Blue," I said, "if I can get into Fayetteville this weekend." This, I thought, would hint to him to stop the conversation soon and leave something for our happy get-together.

"Do that, boy," he persisted. "Did you know Jennie Soanso is in town now? Her family's been here for quite a time—" and on and on and on. I wondered if the flesh of my back had been torn away to the bone yet. True Blue continued.

"Well, True Blue," I moaned, "it sure has been nice hearing from you again—and I'll look you up this weekend." The top sergeant coughed loudly and cleared his throat several times.

"Yep, it's nice to talk with you, boy," said True Blue. "Just like old times. Say, that reminds me! I saw another of the old gang in Charlotte about a month ago. You remember old Jernigan, don't you? Well, do you know what he's doing now?"

I rolled my eyes helplessly at the top kick and started making faces at the telephone mouthpiece. True Blue delivered a complete history of old Jernigan's career since last I had seen him.

"Well, True Blue," I said, "I guess I'll have to go now. I'm sick and sunburned and confined to quarters and I better get back." I was beginning to wonder whether the oilskin was buried completely in my back by this time. Several huge blisters gave up the struggle.

"Let me tell you what happened to—" he began again.

I don't know how the conversation ended. I think the telephone fell out of my hand when I started having my convulsion.

31. THEY'RE DRAFTING HONEST, RESPECT-ABLE, hard-working soldiers back into civilian life now, as you probably read in the papers. Has-beens at twenty-eight, these good boys are turned into the pasture under a selective retirement system. It's interesting to watch the way they take it.

Our big loss in Battery A came Tuesday when Joe

Gantt went back to Liberty, South Carolina, after five months in the citizen army. Joe is the nice corporal who looked like the soldier pictures in the magazines, used an instinctive psychology in handling his men, and knew every man in the battery as a friend.

He was on furlough last week when he was ordered to return at once to the battery. He came back, started through the discharge routine and went about hugging everybody with what looked like unbounded joy.

Then he started getting quieter and less demonstrative. He had been relieved from active duty for the remainder of his stay here—a matter of four or five days—and when the men fell out for calisthenics or drill, Corporal Gantt didn't have to go out with them. Every time the whistle blew, you could see a lonesome look creeping into his eyes.

The last time I saw him was Monday at noon, when we fell out for chow. Military procedure was overthrown in a spontaneous revolution and Joe was drafted to march us to the mess hall. It was his last detail. Halfway to the mess hall, he gave us "To the rear—march! To the right flank—march! To the right flank—march!" and all of the marching commands he had taught us.

He's returning to Liberty now, where he'll fall back easily into the life he left five months ago. But you could have seen from a casual glance that he was going to miss the Army.

Another of the men to be discharged here was "Little David" Rosenthal. Little David, a week before he got his papers, had talked to me in a very despondent manner. He outlined his definite opinion that the men who are now thirty or thirty-odd years old have been systematically given the run-around by Fate. They grew up in the confusion which followed the last war and marched out of high school or the first years of college straight into the teeth of the depression. Then when better times came and they began to find themselves, along came the new war.

The next time I saw him, he had been given his notice. He danced about like a child on Christmas morning, roared gleefully, and went into eloquent Jewish rhetoric to describe his feelings.

"I told them," he shouted, covering his face with an expression of mock grief, "I said to them, 'Please just let me stay until Christmas so I can dig into that turkey. Just until Christmas!'" His voice sank into pathos. "But they wouldn't let me!"

Little David discolored 250 broad backs belonging to the men he pounded to show his joy at returning home. He sat on the barracks steps for hours at a time, beaming blissfully. He was, as our Ussery would say, as happy as a pig in the sunshine.

Then there's the Cisco Kid, who is a student in the same kitchen with me. Cisco is a nice Puerto Rican boy of about thirty. His real name is Weber and he comes from New York City. Even as a mere student, he's one of the best cooks in the Replacement Center.

The Cisco Kid has two brothers, one of whom is in the Army. The other is a boy of twenty-one, who is going to college and holding down a good future-hold-ing job at the same time. The Selective Service System gave him a deferred classification in view of his brothers' present service in the Army. As soon as either brother was released from the service, the boy was to be automatically drafted.

Cisco was notified that he was eligible for discharge, and he began immediately worrying about the kid brother. Whereas Cisco himself was doing well in the Army and was enjoying himself immensely, the brother would find himself and the lovely future temporarily tangled.

The Cisco Kid studied the problem until he had beaten it into dust. He found the solution. He accepted his discharge and immediately volunteered for the thirty-month service period.

32. I'M GETTING TO A POINT where I throw down any magazine which has an article about the draft army. No matter what phase of the life they discuss, I usually get a tired feeling before I finish reading.

An article guaranteed to give me that tired feeling is one, usually written by an oldster who managed to get out of the last war, which stamps and snorts about the sissiness of the draftees and their routine. "These selectees are a bunch of creampuffs who don't know what an army is. They act like Boy Scouts and they're trained and handled as if they were all senators' sons. They aren't soldiers like we were!"

The back of my neck to you, grandfather.

I'm a student cook in the Army. Cooks are supposed to have the easiest work and the most comfortable positions the Army affords. Compared to the boys in the gun batteries, the signal corps, the antitank units, we're almost white-collar men.

We student cooks—the future "happiness" boys of the Army—have to get up for reveille at the usual hour, beating the sun to the rise every morning. We get an hour of calisthenics, directed by a noncom who's in good physical shape and expects us to be the same way. Then we drill for an hour, and hell hath no fury like that unleashed on the recreant who doesn't come up to standard in drill. We attend class for two hours and there's no foolishness there.

After lunch, we report to our kitchens, where we work until seven o'clock, taking our trade practically, taking part in the preparation of food for over two hundred hungry and fastidious soldiers. The next morning finds us in our kitchen at three or four o'clock and we stay there until one. We're supposed to have the afternoon off—unless there's something that has to be done in the line of battery duty.

When we leave those kitchens for the afternoon, we go back to our barracks for rest and sleep, which we need badly after the twenty-four-hour shift at huge coal-burning stoves. Reading is a popular diversion during the time, unless you pick up a magazine which tells you what slackers you are because you aren't like the author was in the Real war.

Then there's another altogether different type of article that is equally nauseating. It tells of the poor little soldier boys, who give up everything to go into training thousands of miles from mother's lap and who will have to spend their time leaning against urban lampposts—because nothing is being done for their morale.

You're talking about entertainment, Gertrude—not morale. In the matter of entertainment, there's plenty of that to be found, even if it isn't like being back home toasting marshmallows with Her. There's so much being done here for entertainment that you can't get halfway to the Service Club without being drafted for a battery show or a volleyball game.

Morale, to my way of thinking, is not a matter of entertainment. It isn't a feeling that fills you when you play spin-the-bottle.

Morale is the spirit that gets you when you're out on the regimental parade ground with the whole battalion for retreat parade. Every mother's son there wants to look as much the soldier as the Old Man does. Not another sound can be heard before or after the one-gun salute to the colors or when the band crosses the field to a stirring march in the Display of the Colors. And when your battery passes in review before the colonel, you're firmly convinced that there isn't another battery on the field that makes as good a showing as your battery.

It's the enormous feeling you know when you sit in pitch dark before a pup tent in the field and watch the fort's searchlight cut the sky. It's the feeling you know when you can look across a great space and see long lines of Army trucks moving along every road you can see.

That's morale. Just a matter of pride.

33. THE GOOD EARTH ON WHICH FORT BRAGG is situated is laden with tradition, ghosts of the glorious past, the old culture—and little else. Beautiful as it may be for purposes of military training, it has little interest in helping the little green things to grow. Grass and flowers, planted with loving care in the Sandhills dust, fade but too soon if left to shift for themselves. To nourish such vegetation, the cavalry units furnish the more aesthetic batteries with certain surplus commodities.

Private McGlauflin, Roff, and I had spent the better part of the morning with Corporal Cleveland James Farmer, heaving and hauling coal in preparation for the long hard winter, when the top sergeant decided that the borders around the barracks should be given their autumn tonic. We piled back into our truck and sped away to the haunts of the hoss cavalry.

We knew, after a few miles of riding, that we were nearing the cavalry territory. There was a certain unmistakable quality about the atmosphere. Something New Had Been Added.

The hoss cavalry, it must be said, takes great pains with the care and distribution of its vitamin deposits. As far as the eye can see the eye can see orderly, cubical mounds covered with straw and earth. None but the most deserving criminal offenders—men who have earned their letter ("P" for "prisoner") are permitted to serve in the maintenance division of this essential agricultural enterprise. None but the most vigilant guards are permitted to supervise their labors.

We three—McGlauflin, Roff, and I—stood high on the crest of a hill, loading the truck with its precious cargo, commenting on the invigorating quality of the air, and pausing ever and anon to lean on our pitchforks and listen to the conversation of other workers about us.

Some there were who could not see the importance of the service they were rendering; others spoke disparagingly of the place and bitterly cursed man's best friend, the horse. Two soldiers who shared a single pitchfork at the next truck spent all their time discussing the comparative beauties of the music of Liszt and Tchaikovsky, proving that art endureth forever even in an alien atmosphere.

As for myself, I gloried in the honor of the tradition I was helping to carry out. My mind drew pictures of

the philosopher Ward Beecher Threatt, who boasts
that he carried a pitchfork through the heat of the
fiercest battles throughout the last war.

Corporal Farmer had no comment to make about the
work. Himself a philosopher, he feels that a job worth
doing is worth doing right.

We made three trips to the cavalry barnyard before
we had finished enriching the earth about the orderly
room, the mess hall, and the four barracks of Battery A.
We bathed vigorously and dressed for early dinner.

The mess sergeant met us at the door. He sniffed the
air delicately and quietly closed the door in our faces.
Then he made the rounds, closing the windows nearest
us. "Git!" he said.

We went back to the barracks, where we found our
comrades returned from the classroom. We sat down
on our foot lockers and strove to remain as inconspicuous as possible. Private Sher was the first to speak.

"Do you smell something?" Private Sher asked with
unaccustomed rudeness. Everyone, it seemed, smelled
something. It was not, they decided, Chanel Number
Five. It was not My Sin or Evening in Paris. One of
the citizen-soldiers, who had once worked in the stock-
yards, knew what it was.

When the hunt came nearer, Privates McGlauflin,
Roff, and I arose and quietly left the squadroom and
quietly sat by the newly invigorated grass borders
outside.

We are social outcasts for the time. We are shunned
by our fellows and driven from the circle of polite

society. But spring will come, nature will unfold its loveliest treasures. And grass will grow, green and resplendent, in the borders of Battery A.

34. MAYBE I SPOKE TOO SOON when I denied the sissiness charges by magazine writers. It must be admitted, after yesterday's horrible disclosure, that some termite is boring from within us. Some force is sapping the rugged manliness of Battery A.

Here's what happened at supper yesterday evening. First of all, when we neared the end of the chow line, we found one of the cooks there, scooping ice cream out of a can. We are meat-and-potato men in Battery A and generally we do not take to such frilly fanciness as ice cream, although we occasionally humor the mess sergeant by letting him buy it in ready-cut blocks.

This time, we found, he had gone too far. Our leniency and tolerance in letting him buy ice cream had gone to his head. Now he was making it at home— in the respectable kitchen of Battery A! Homemade pineapple ice cream!

I didn't say anything about it. I thought that perhaps he was merely going through his second childhood, and second childhood is something that every mess sergeant must be permitted to go through once. Realizing this, we boys hadn't said anything when our mess sergeant had air-conditioning fans put in the kitchen windows to make namby-pambies of the cooks and kaypees. We hadn't said anything when he started keeping jam on the table at all meals.

We're going to have to say something now. The man is going absolutely mad. Not content with springing homemade ice cream on us, he had to heap more coals on the fire of our impatience at the same meal.

There on each table in our mess hall, brazenly placed in the very center, was a shiny container filled with paper napkins!

Until something is done about the thing, this mess sergeant will go hog-wild. At his present rate, we'll find toothpicks on the table next week, salad forks the week after that, finger bowls before November.

This will go on indefinitely until his brain is completely destroyed by this madness. Then he'll start planning to surprise us with waitresses dressed in field-artillery red.

When this happens, I shall try to volunteer for the parachute troops.

LINGERIE NOTE: Our winter uniforms were issued to us today and, since we had the afternoon off, we spent all our time until retreat trying on the pretties and parading before each other. The clothes were all all-wool and the temperature was all-heat, but all was vanity.

We knew what the trousers, shirts, ties, blouses, and

overcoats would look like, but the remainder of the wardrobe came as a complete surprise to us. We were especially intrigued by the woolen gloves and the pretty gray-blue socks.

But the pièce de résistance was the underwear, if I may be indelicate. Private Huber and some of the other less fortunate citizen-soldiers were issued simple, unglamorous longies in a color that could best be described as lemon custard. The cut of these pale beauties was the orthodox, one-piece design such as one sees hung on the washlines of all comic strips.

But the others—the ones like I got! Such empty, inadequate things as words can never describe these garments. They are subjects for a more graphic art.

From wrist to ankle, we will be clothed this winter in two-piece ensembles of a color halfway between baby blue and rabbit gray. The undershirts are cut on a sweat-shirt pattern and are form fitting enough to send any Hollywood designer into frenzies of envy. The nether garments, which are called "shorts" for some unfathomable reason, look like the tights worn in medieval days and show off the shapeliness of a masculine leg to best advantage—or otherwise.

I like mine so well I'm going to have pictures made of me in them. Won't the boys back home be jealous!

35. NO MATTER HOW HOMEY they make the Service Clubs, no matter how carefully they plan the movie programs, no matter how hard they work on athletic schedules, they'll never be able to compete with a soldier's favorite evening recreation—sitting on the back steps, shooting the breeze.

By this time, the evening bull sessions have worn themselves into a very definite routine. If Corporal Ussery is there, he lectures on how he'd run the Army; if it's Private Terence Clarkin, he tells how he used to direct the intricate traffic affairs of Radio City Music Hall when he was assistant chief doorman there. Unless Private Henri Gelders is stopped, he'll start a violent argument among the butchers over how to cut a steak.

McGlauflin will talk for hours about the beauties of the lakes in Minnesota. Grafenstein will deliver discourses on how he would run the Wisconsin football team; Pappas, about Alabama's Crimson Tide. Maciejewski will sermonize on the utter baseness and treachery of womanhood.

Lately, however, the sessions have come more and more under the sway of Private Merton Hulce, a mad Irish lad from Muskegon, Michigan. Private Hulce apparently didn't stop at kissing the Blarney Stone. He must have stolen half of it to carry with him.

Hulce's chief topic of conversation is his mother's fabulous family, the Smiths, all of whom seem to get enmeshed in every war that comes along. His grand-father, who was a captain in the Coast Guard at the outbreak of the last war, was transferred to duty at guarding munitions dumps and such for the duration of the war.

According to Hulce, one of the munitions guards with his grandfather's detail was approached late one night by an officer of the guard. "Halt!" shouted the sentry, and the officer halted. "Advance to be recognized!" said the sentry, and the officer advanced. The sentry forgot to order "halt" again and the officer came within a foot of him. Suddenly the officer reached out and snatched the rifle from the guard's hand.

This was an exceedingly uncomfortable position for the guard, especially in that time of war. He might even have been sentenced to death. The officer stood there just looking at the guard for fully a minute. "What would you have done," he asked in a terrible voice, "if an enemy had got your gun like that?"

The guard trembled for a moment and recovered. "I would have snatched it back, sir," he said, "like THAT!" And the officer stood there, empty-handed.

Hulce's grandfather, who told that story, is now about sixty-five, his grandson says. He was asked to come back into the Navy three months ago as a captain. Being a Smith, he's back. With him in the armed forces today are two of his sons and two of his grandsons.

Merton had two uncles in the last war, both of whom fared exceedingly well when you take a practical view of it. Neither tired himself out. The first crossed the ocean nine times playing the clarinet in a troop ship's band. The Germans torpedoed the boat once and the holes in the side were stuffed with mattresses. Hulce's uncle rode back into port, still playing his clarinet. That was the goldbricking uncle.

The other uncle served as a kaypee on the trip across. Carrying a tray around the deck, he was heckled several times by a person he soon grew to loathe. Eventually the Irish wrath of the Smiths rose to boiling point. Uncle Smith lifted the tray high overhead and wrapped it around the heckler's neck. He spent the rest of the war in confinement.

Then there was the cousin, grandma's sister's boy. Serving in the front-line trenches, he grew suddenly hungry one morning. Looking out of the trench, he saw a peach tree growing there in the midst of the fiery hell, and there were still peaches on it. He tried to sneak into the tree, but the enemy's bullets found him. He was carried behind the lines. Just as the stretcher bearers laid him down, an enemy shell exploded in the center of their little group and none of them were ever seen again.

This happened at exactly ten o'clock on the morning of November 11, 1918—one hour before the Armistice was signed.

36. NEXT TO THE BUGLER, I suppose the battery clerk has the goldbrickin'est job in the battery. You could cut his pay to ten dollars a month and he'd still be defrauding the government.

Just watch the battery clerk for a while and you start wondering why he's in the Army, when he's so evidently cut out to fit the leaning end of a WPA shovel. While the rest of the battery is earning its daily bread with sweat, the battery clerk sits in the orderly room hobnobbing with the powers that be, typing the daily worklist with original spellings for all the names and wondering how long it is until lunchtime.

Our battery clerk is a beardless youth named Howard Miller, who did his daily stint of loafing behind the Yankee lines in Cincinnati before he got his corporal's stripes.

I tripped over him yesterday evening on my way back from a hard day's work and stopped to chew the conversational fat. Talk offers the only outlet for a battery clerk's otherwise unused energy.

"Junior," I asked him, "how does your conscience feel about this six-day goldbricking schedule every week? Don't you feel a twinge on payday?"

Corporal Miller made a move to draw himself up indignantly, but decided it wasn't worth the effort. "If you're insinuating that I don't have to work you're off your bean, sonny. I do two or three times as much work as you happiness boys."

I yawned and sat down. "After listening to Ussery shooting off his mouth fifteen hours a day, I can take yours. Go on with your fantastic story."

"Boy," said Miller, "the responsibility is enough to kill an ordinary man. I'm a one-man information bureau for the whole battery. I have to know who everybody is, where everybody is, where everybody's going and how long he's going to be there.

"I have to know the answer to every dumb question you guys come popping up with. Where's my mail? When do I get my furlough? Where are we going to be sent when we get shipped out of here? Why didn't I get a weekend pass? Why was I on KP again today? Every sort of question you could imagine!"

"Quit popping your gums, laddie," I told him. "That's no grind for you. You use the same answer on all the questions: 'How the hell would I know?'"

He was quiet for a while and I thought he had gone to sleep again. I was all primed to hum "Chow Call" to wake him up, when he stirred and sighed heavily.

"All right," I prompted him, "so you're the one-man information bureau. So what do you do in the line of actual work?"

"Work!" he shouted. "That's what I do—work! Why, I have to write all the letters and keep all the files and keep duty rosters up to date! I have to make thousands of rosters of the battery every month—"

"Thousands?" I asked gently.

"I said hundreds," he said. I could have beaten him down to dozens.

"That," I suggested, "should take at least two or three hours every day. What do you do to while away the other tedious hours of the day?"

He was quiet again for about a minute. Then he arose. "I've got a pretty hard day ahead of me tomorrow, Hargrove," he said. "I hope you won't mind if you excuse myself. You have to get plenty of sleep when you have a job like mine."

"When you have a job like yours," I growled, "you can sleep night and day."

Next to the bugler, I suppose the battery clerk has the goldbrickin'est job. You could cut his pay to ten dollars a month and he'd still be defrauding the government.

37. THE TOP SERGEANT STUCK his head out of the supply room and beckoned with his arm. "Come 'ere, you!"

I dropped my stable broom in the battery street and hastened toward him, as one always does when summoned by the top kick.

"Well, Private Hargrove," he said, "this is a red-letter day for you."

"You mean you're going to let me go out and drill like the other fellows?"

"Noooo, Private Hargrove," he said. "I mean I'm going to let you turn in all your equipment. You are no longer to be a rookie, Private Hargrove. You are going to be an important working cog in the great wheel of national defense. You are leaving us, Private Hargrove."

I leaned against a filing cabinet to figure it out.

"You should be very happy, Private Hargrove," he said tenderly. "I thought you would have been in this three-month training cycle for at least six years. You make me proud of you."

"What's the deal?" I asked. "Where do I go and what do I do?"

The sergeant chuckled and leaned back in his chair. He sighed ecstatically twice. "Would you really like to know, son, or would you rather put it off as long as you can?"

"Well," I said thankfully, "you can't be sending me out as a cook, because I don't know anything about cooking."

The sergeant sat back and drummed happily on the table.

"Great gods!" I shouted. "I'm not going to be a cannoneer, am I?"

The top sergeant rocked back and forth on the hind legs of his chair and hummed half a chorus of "Maple on the Hill" (No. 2). "No, Private Hargrove," he said after another long pause, "you're not going to be a cannoneer. We're going to give you a job where you can use your natural talents."

There was a distinctly sadistic tone in his voice. I waited.

"You're going to be a first cook, Hargrove," he said fondly. "Not just a plain cook. A head cook! A king in your own kitchen, a man of responsibility. Ain't that lovely?"

I was appalled. I clawed silently for air while Sergeant Goldsmith resumed his soft humming of "Maple on the Hill" (No. 2).

"You can't do this to me!" I roared, when my breath returned. "It's against every decent human law! I don't know anything about cooking! I want to be a cannoneer!"

Sergeant Goldsmith's eyes wandered guilelessly to the ceiling. "You don't know anything about cooking, huh? That's bad, boy, that's bad! Why, you're supposed to be on shift right now."

"Sergeant," I said, "I couldn't fry an egg right now if it had directions on the package."

"You're in the cooks' battery, ain't you? You've been going to cooking school and you've been sent to a kitchen for all these weeks. You're supposed to be graduated any day now. What have you been doing in the kitchen I put you in?"

"Making jerk-ade," I explained, "chopping celery, peeling onions. They say I get in their way. They say I keep spirits too high and production too low."

"I feel for you," the sergeant said. "I deeply sympathize. You're going to be a mighty unpopular little boy in your new home. If that supper tonight don't melt in them boys' mouths and send them clamoring for more, they'll either massacre you or run you over the hill. That's one thing the boys won't allow—bum cooking!"

"Sergeant Goldsmith, sir," I implored him, "can't somebody else go in my stead? Somebody who can cook? Look at me—a digger of ditches, a mopper of floors, a scrubber of kitchens, a ministering angel to undernourished grass plots, but a cook never! You don't know what you're doing to me!"

The top kick looked dreamily through the orderly-room door. "Son," he said, "you're going to make a perfectly breath-taking Horrible Example!"

I had nothing more to say. The sergeant crossed his right foot over his left knee and sat watching a fly on the window screen. He took a cigarette from his pocket, lighted it and settled back into reverie.

Then he rose and walked back into the supply room. "Thomas," he said, "check in this yardbird's equipment."

Sergeant Israel looked up from his Form Thirty-Two records. "Don't he like his equipment?"

"Check in everything but his clothing," the top kick said. "Get a truck to take him to Headquarters Battery, FARC."

Sergeant Thomas W. Israel looked up in faint amazement. I looked in sheer bewilderment.

"They had to figure some way to stop his cooking

career and save the morale of some battery as would get him as a cook," said Sergeant Goldsmith. "So he's being palmed off to Center Headquarters as a public relations man."

"The Lord giveth," said Sergeant Israel, "and the Lord taketh away."

"Blessed be the name of the Lord," said the top kick.

38. THE WORD "BUDDY" hasn't come into popularity yet in the new army. I suppose that if there were such things, Maury Sher would be mine. Sher and I occupied adjoining bunks when I was in Battery A. I bummed most of my cigarettes from him and we always got into trouble together.

Private Sher is a smart and likable Jewish boy from Columbus, Ohio. He went to school at Southern California, until he learned that all the world's knowledge doesn't come from the intellectual invalids who usually teach the 8:30 class. Then he went back to Columbus, had an idea patented, and built himself a restaurant shaped like a champagne glass.

Came the fateful Sixteenth of October and Sher enrolled for the Selective Service System. His application was accepted last July and, since he had been the successful proprietor of a restaurant, he was classified as a promising student for the Army cooking course.

The two of us got together when he was sent to the Replacement Center here. We started an acquaintance when I topped all his Jewish jokes and began teaching him how to speak Yiddish. I was attracted by his native intelligence, his pleasant personality, his sense of humor, the similarity of his likes and dislikes to mine, his subscription to *PM,* his well-stocked supply of cigarettes (my brand), and the cookies he constantly received from home.

So we became more or less constant companions. We made the rounds here together, went to Charlotte together, made goo-goo eyes at the same waitress in Fayetteville, and swapped valuable trade secrets in goldbricking.

There was one Sunday evening when Sher started a letter to his family and found, after a couple of paragraphs, that there was nothing for him to write about. "Here, Junior," he said. "Write a letter for your old daddy. Give them the old Hargrovian schmaltz."

Since Junior was in a devilish mood, he sat down and wrote a long and inspired letter to the Shers of Columbus, Ohio—telling them how their little Maurice was falling behind in his classes by goldbricking and hanging out late at the Service Club, entreating them to return him to his true career, the Army. I finished by saying, "You see who's writing the letters; you should know where to send the cookies. Forget that bum Maury."

Several days later—after I had swapped my skillet for a typewriter and had moved to Headquarters Battery—I came by Battery A to see if I had any mail from my nonwriting friends in Charlotte. There weren't any letters, but there was a package which looked about the size of a steamer trunk. There were enough cookies inside to feed a small regiment for three days.

The card inside read: "Dear Hargrove—We think your idea about the cookies is superb. Give Maury one or two; he's a good boy when he wants to be. Why don't you come up to Columbus on your furlough?"

It seemed that this beautiful friendship—with all its fragrant memories, its happy hours of hell-raising, its beautiful cigarettes, cookies, and Samaritan relatives—was destined to end with the closing of the basic training cycle here.

I had already left Battery A for another residential section a half mile away. We managed to get together three or four times a week for a movie, a trip to Fayetteville, or a pleasant evening of bull-shooting at the Service Club. But even this was to pass.

Sher's own thirteen weeks were drawing to a close and he was slated to be assigned to a permanent station as a cook. With sinking hearts, we watched group after group leave for camps in Louisiana, Georgia, Missouri, New York, Michigan.

And then pleasant news came over the grapevine telegraph. Private Maurice Sher, by reason of skill, application, and neatness, had been assigned as a cook for the Center Headquarters officers' mess.

It's only latrine gossip, but if it comes through it means that Private Sher will be transferred to Headquarters Battery and the team of Hargrove and Sher will ride again.

39. THE OLD GANG, which has lived and worked and played together for over three months and has grown into a close and sympathetic brotherhood, is dissolving now. The training cycle is being finished and already the old ties are loosing.

The student cooks whom I grew to know and feel a fondness for during those months are not so fortunate as some of the other soldiers. The Charlotte boys who were inducted with me and who went through their antitank training together will go together to Fort Knox and will continue to be with each other for at least a little while. On the other hand, these student cooks of Battery A will not go out together. No fort is going to be sent a whole battery of cooks. One cook will be needed here, another there, and the old third platoon will be scattered from hell to breakfast.

An old thirty-year man, with five or six hash marks on his sleeve, will tell you that no matter how long you stay in the Army, you'll never find a battery that quite stacks up to the first battery in which you served, no group of buddies quite like the old gang you knew first.

There's a reason for it. In your first organization, you learn for the first time all the regulations and the customs and the traditions of the Army. When you first face them, they're tough or they're uninteresting, and when you finally get to understand and agree with them, they're identified in your memory with the battery where you learned them.

With the men who serve with you there, you grow closer through hardship and privation than you can possibly grow to any other group. After you get out into a line organization—a real tactical unit, such as these boys are entering—any hardship or misery is just a part of the routine. The sufferers are men rather than boys.

But in this first training cycle, this rookie stage, you haven't been hardened. You and the new soldiers about you are sensitive, delicate boys, newly yanked from home or school, accustomed to an easygoing and usually painless life. You share each other's illness, fatigue, despair. When Happy Menza grows homesick for Buffalo and McGlauflin starts a wistful reminiscing about the lakes and forests of Minnesota, you are homesick for them rather than for yourself. You are companions tested in misery.

Friday night was probably the last evening the boys of my old crowd would be together. At least, it was the last evening they were sure of being together. The following day they were to go home for a week's furlough. On their return, next Monday, they will be assigned to their permanent stations to enter the field as soldiers. So they arranged to hold a party Friday night on the river beyond Fayetteville.

When we rode to the river in our chartered bus, we rang the welkin with the old songs—the faintly fragrant songs you pick up through the years and the "Caisson Song" and "Old King Cole" that you learn in the Army. They were boisterous, those songs, but a melancholy strain ran under all of them.

At the party we ate barbecue and we drank beer and we recalled the best anecdotes of the training cycle. We sang and we shouted. Two or three of the boys dipped a little too deep into the keg and became slightly sentimental. And although the food and the beer were the best, the songs were the songs we loved and the anecdotes were the cream of the season, it was empty joy. It had a dull undercurrent of sorrow.

It was the sort of feeling that you know in the last hour before the New Year's bells, the feeling that reaches its fullest when "Auld Lang Syne" is heard.

Since we left our homes last July we've learned a lot. Drills and rifles, pup tents and gas masks, all of that.

This, though—the scattering of our first fraternity— is another thing we have learned, now and for the first time. It is our first lesson in a new kind of homesickness, bred only in the Army.

40. "PRIVATE HARGROVE," I SAID to myself, "you have been doing quite too much gallivanting lately. There have been too many movies, too many bull sessions, too many hours spent at the Service Club and too much time spent flirting with that cute little waitress at the delicatessen in Fayetteville. Tonight, Private Hargrove, you will take this interesting and improving book, read it until Lights Out and go to bed promptly at nine o'clock."

There was a little back talk, a little argument, a little entreaty. However, the forces of Truth and Progress prevailed. Immediately after supper I adjourned to the squadroom, arranged myself comfortably on my bunk and dug into the interesting book. Peace and quiet held sway about me.

As luck would have it, this same sudden decision toward a Quiet Evening at Home struck several fellow members of the squadroom at the same time. Six or seven near-by bunks sported occupants who usually disdained the comforts of home until at least nine o'clock. Books were brought out from the foot lockers, pens and papers made their appearance, and one ambitious and energetic flower of the nation even got out his shoe polish and went to work.

Private Wesley Sager, late of Amsterdam, New York, grew weary of the quiet. Yawning widely, he rolled over in bed and with a sudden swoop yanked the pillow from beneath the head of Private Melvin Hart. "Yip-pee," screamed Private Sager, tossing the pillow across the squadroom to a willing accomplice. "Yippee," screamed the willing accomplice, tossing the pillow back to Private Sager.

Private Hart rose and retrieved his pillow with dignity and formality. He placed it on his bunk, smoothed it and laid his head upon it. Three privates sighed in resignation. The incorrigibles were at it again.

Private Sager lay quiet for a while. Then he broke into a loud, regular, but unconvincing snore. The three sighing privates did not return to their occupations, but lay in philosophic expectation. Once the boys in that corner got started, nothing but physical exhaustion could stop them.

Private Sager turned as if tossing in his sleep. Private Hart noted the move and held his book ready to strike if a hand came toward his pillow. Private Sager turned again, facing away from Private Hart, and Private Hart relaxed his vigil. When he did, the hand shot out once more and the pillow sailed across the room and into waiting arms.

Again Private Hart retrieved the pillow and again he lay down. "Why," he asked, "must you behave like a two-year-old infant? Can't you act like a normal adult?"

"Sure I can," Private Sager replied. "Kindly step outside with me and put up your fists."

Private Hart gave vent to a quiet and gentlemanly oath. "Please do me the honor to shut your mouth," he requests. "I should like to read without the clamor of your big yap roaring in my ears."

This is but the opening gun. Almost daily it marks the beginning of a half-hour session of blusters, threats, extravagantly insulting remarks, and repeated invitations from each side for the other to step outside and settle it. Nothing ever comes of it and soon the contending parties tire of the play.

Silence reigns again, but its throne is shaky. Private Hart tires of his book and turns to Private Sager. "Were you at the dance last night when that redhead got started telling what she thought of Jim Carney's dancing?"

Private Carney picks up the bait. "Anything Hart says about me or about what anybody else says about me is entirely fictitious, and any resemblance to persons living or dead is coincidental and not intended."

Private Sager sits up suddenly in bed. "Don't talk like that about Hart," he says in a quiet, serious, and menacing voice. "Anything you say about Hart is a personal insult to me. If you're inclined to insult me, kindly take off your stripe and step outside with me."

"Don't you go talking like that to the ranking first-class private of this section," rasps Private Hart. "I don't like your manner at all. Kindly step outside with me while I beat your brains out."

Thus it goes.

If you want peace and quiet on these stay-at-home nights, the best solution is to go to the second barracks down the line. There's nobody down there except fifty-eight members of the band, who are always rehearsing at this time of night.

41. "THE THING THAT WORRIES ME about the Army today," said the Ex-Service Man, "is the lack of enthusiasm the soldier of today puts into his griping. What's the matter with them?

"Last weekend in Charlotte, I spent the better part of a night ferrying boys to the sleeping places around town and every time I'd ask a couple of them how they liked the Army and how they were getting along in it, they'd smile and say, 'Oh, just fine, thank you' or something like that. The whole night I ran across only two of them who put their heart and soul into their griping. Just two of them, mind you. They were real, rip-snorting, cussing, and fuming gripers—the genuine old-time soldier.

"What's the matter with the rest of them? Are they against bellyaching, or has bellyaching just gone out of fashion as an indoor sport?"

"The only answer I can give you," I told him, "is that the boys you talked with were tired and sleepy or they just had on their company manners. The average Selective Service man can gripe just as well as the old

World War veteran. What's more, he has the advantage of twenty or twenty-five years' improvement in the technique."

To enlarge upon the point, I dug into my pockets and came out with a letter that had been going the rounds at the Replacement Center. To my mind, it's a classic example of soldierly griping. Here it is:

"Dear, unfortunate civilian friend: I am very enthusiastic about Army life. We lie around in bed every morning until at least six o'clock. This, of course, gives us plenty of time to get washed and dressed and make the bunks, etc., by 6:10. At 6:15 we stand outside and shiver while some (deleted) blows a bugle. After we are reasonably chilled, we grope our way through the darkness to the mess hall. Here we have a hearty breakfast consisting of an unidentified liquid and a choice of white or rye crusts.*

"After gorging ourselves with this delicious repast, we waddle our way back to the barracks. We have nothing to do until 7:30 so we just sit around and scrub toilets, mop the floors, wash the windows and pick up all the matchsticks and cigarette butts within a radius of 2,000 feet of the barracks.

"Soon the sergeant comes in and says, 'Come out in the sunshine, kiddies!' So we go out and bask in the wonderful North Carolina sunshine—of course, we stand knee-deep in the wonderful North Carolina sand.

---

* This is the only really weak spot of the letter. The average soldier does his best griping about food, and the more weight he gains therefrom the more he gripes.—Hargrove.

To limber up, we do a few simple calisthenics, such as touching your toes with both feet off the ground and grabbing yourself by the hair and holding yourself at arm's length.

"At 8 o'clock we put on our light packs and go for a tramp in the hills. The light pack includes gun, bayonet, canteen, fork, knife, spoon, meat can, cup, shaving kit, pup tent, raincoat, cartridge belt, first-aid kit, fire extinguisher, tent pins, rope, tent pole, hand ax, small spade, and a few other negligible items. Carrying my light pack, I weigh 217¼ pounds. I weighed 131 pounds when I left home, so you can see how easy it is to gain weight in the Army.

"An observation car follows us as we climb the hills and picks up the fellows who faint. The boys who fall out in the mountain climbing are treated very well. They are given six months in the guardhouse, but they don't have to face court-martial. At twelve o'clock those who can, limp to the infirmary. At the infirmary, patients are divided into two classes: (1) those who have athlete's foot, and (2) those who have colds. If you have athlete's foot, you get your feet swabbed with iodine. If you have a cold, you get your throat swabbed with iodine. Anyone who claims he has neither a cold nor athlete's foot is sent to the guardhouse for impersonating an officer.

"I am very popular at the infirmary. I told them that I have both a cold and athlete's foot. What I really have is gastric ulcers, but I know when to keep my mouth shut.

"Well, that's all I have to write, as I hear the call for chow and I don't want to get there late. You see, tonight they have hominy for supper and I don't want to lose out on a treat like that. Hominy again—oh, boy!

"P.S. Definition for hominy: French-fried moth-balls."

42. SLANG RUNS WILD in the Army. It's like a disease or the liquor habit. Among the boys who sit around on the back steps after Lights Out and bat the breeze far into the night, no simple and understandable English word is used where a weird and outlandish concoction can be substituted. After collecting them for a few weeks on the backs of old dunning letters, here's what I find:

The subject of food calls for a brutal mutilation of the language. Probably there is more slang associated with the mess hall than with the accumulated remainder of the Army.

Water is *GI lemonade*. Salt is *sand* or *Lot's wife;* pepper is *specks;* sugar is *sweetening compound*. Milk is *cat beer;* butter, *dogfat*. Ketchup is *blood*. In the untiring imagination of the soldier, green peas become *China berries;* hominy grits are glamorized into *Geor-*

gia ice cream; rice is *swamp seed.* Potatoes become *Irish grapes;* prunes change to *strawberries;* hot cakes become *blankets.* Bread is *punk* and creamed beef on toast is *punk and salve.* Meat loaf and hash are *kennel rations.*

It is strictly against the code of the Army to say a complimentary word about the food or the cook, no matter how good the food is or how hard the cook labors to make it so. Oscar of the Waldorf, in the Army, would still be either a *slum-burner* or a *belly-robber.*

Back at the *News,* the boys in the composing room and the mailing department used to send greenhorns searching all over the building for erasing ink, striped or dotted ink, paper stretchers, and other nonexistent items. Here, a new and gullible man is sent for the *cannon report,* or for the *biscuit gun,* the *flagpole key,* or the *rubber flag* which is used on rainy days.

Here are some of the most popular figures of speech:

Army Bible—the Articles of War; regulations.

Barrage—a party, especially where the Demon Rum rears its ugly head.

Blanket drill—sleep.

Butchershop—a dispensary or hospital.

By the numbers—like clockwork; with precision and efficiency.

Chili bowl—regulation haircut.

Chest hardware—medals.

Didie pins—the gold bars of a second lieutenant.

Dog robber—an orderly.

The eagle—money. On payday, *the eagle flies.*

Front and center—come forward.

Flying time—sleep.

Gashouse—a beer joint.

Glue—honey.

Goof off—to make a mistake.

Handshaking—playing up to superiors.

Higher brass—the higher ranks of officers.

Hollywood corporal—an acting corporal.

Holy Joe—the chaplain.

Honey wagon—the garbage truck.

Housewife—a soldier's sewing kit.

Jubilee—reveille, which is too often pronounced "revelee."

Mother Machree—a sob-story alibi.

Pocket lettuce—paper money.

Pontoon checks—canteen checks, good for credit at the post exchange.

Ride the sickbook—to goldbrick the easy way by pretending to be ill.

Shoulder hardware—the shoulder insignia of a commissioned officer.

Sugar report—a letter from the romantic interest back home.

Wailing wall—the chaplain's office.

Windjammer—the bugler.

Milton, thou shouldst be living at this hour!

43. CARL W. MORGAN IS FIRST SERGEANT OF Battery D, Fifth Battalion, Second Training Regiment. I dropped in to see him the other day, to get some information for a story on the battalion's all-selectee review, and we got into a long conversation. The sergeant, I found, was one of the most interesting men in the Replacement Center.

"I was going up to New York on a furlough a little while back," he said, "and while I was waiting to change trains in Richmond, I noticed two soldiers standing on the platform. Both of them were neat as a pin, sober and well-behaved, just standing there minding their own business. I looked at them and I could tell they were good boys and good soldiers. I've been in the business ever since the Mexican expedition days and I ought to know good soldiers when I see them.

"Well, while they were standing there, some fellow came prancing up to them and started raising hell with them. Mind you, they hadn't done a thing. He just wanted to insult them. He degraded them with every low name and nasty remark he could think of—and they just stood there. Neither of them cussed back at him or lifted a hand. They tried not to pay him any mind.

"I got on the train and this guy took the seat right in front of me. I had on civilian clothes, so he didn't know I was a soldier. He turned around to me, knowing

I had heard the conversation, and said he guessed he'd told them proper.

" 'Yes,' I told him, 'you did. And it's a crying shame one of them didn't forget himself and his uniform long enough to slap your teeth down your throat.' Then I proceeded to tell him what I thought of him and his little uncalled-for jump on those two boys. There they were, giving up all that time to learning how to fight to defend him, and there he was, trying to make himself look big by snapping at their heels in public. I told him off proper. He finally got up and left the car before I got started good.

"An old gentleman across the aisle looked over and smiled after the fellow left. 'I'm Colonel —— of the infantry,' he said. 'You certainly shut him up.'

" 'I'm First Sergeant Morgan of the field artillery,' I told him, 'and I'd like to have told him more, sir. I've fought in Mexico, China and God alone knows where else, but I haven't met many men who'd take much of that sort of stuff without pushing the guy's face in.'

"At a time like this, Hargrove, I can't understand the attitude some people take toward the soldiers. No appreciation at all. Here's a nice, clean-living boy. Everybody around knows he's a nice fellow and they all like him. He's just getting a start in the world.

"Then, all of a sudden, hell busts loose and the boy has to drop everything and go to camp. Right then and there, these little cockroaches start looking on him like he was a step or two below them in every way. Thank

God there aren't many people like the fellow in the railroad station, but as long as there's any at all there's too many.

"You know, another thing that's bad on the soldiers now is: You take three or four hundred soldiers and you're going to find some of them getting drunk or fighting or getting into some kind of trouble. Law of averages. Right then and there, the whole bunch are classed as drunkards and brawlers. The percentage isn't as high among soldiers as it is in everyday civilian life, but the uniform makes a soldier conspicuous. One soldier getting drunk attracts more attention than ten civilians doing the same thing.

"You take a bunch of soldiers going into a town for, say, three or four months. Just let three or four get out of line—three or four, mind you—and the town's down on the whole bunch. It just doesn't make sense.

"I've been in this man's army for over a quarter of a century and I know how it is, boy. It's going to take a shooting war to make some people give their soldiers a break."

44. IT'S ENOUGH TO DRIVE A MAN TO DRINK. You get a ten-day furlough and head for New York. You mooch a due bill on an ultra-swank hotel. You say to yourself that for those ten days you will be an all-out civilian, you will squander your substance in riotous living, you will forget altogether the fact that you are a soldier. And then what happens?

You wake up at six o'clock, no matter how late you stay out the night before. Then you can't go back to sleep. You have to buy enormous quantities of civilian food to keep up with your Army appetite. You look in shop windows and see books you'd give your wisdom teeth for, but you think of your purse in terms of $36 a month and the inner man convinces you that you can't afford them.

You'd like very much to put on your civilian clothes, just for a change, but your friends think you look so pretty in your uniform that they won't let you pull the old blue serge out of the mothballs.

It isn't bad all the way through, though.

For instance, I walked out of the hotel the other day and ran into one of the boys from my own barracks, in New York on a three-day pass. We exchanged the prescribed comments on the smallness of the world and I saw a sparkling opportunity to spread a thick layer of hokum. I could make the lad think that I was one of these filthy-rich privates you so often read about in the papers. The kind that go about flashing $1,000 bills before unsuspecting headwaiters.

"Won't you have lunch with me?" I asked. Then I added, quite casually, "I'm stopping here at the Astor."

His eyes popped faintly, but a good soldier never

passes up a free meal. We went back into the hotel
and into the terrifyingly smart dining room. I smiled
condescendingly at the headwaiter, to make him think
I was a cash customer at the hotel, and he led us to a
table.

"I'm afraid you'll find the food here depressingly
'dull,' I told my comrade-in-arms. "No ortolans or
hummingbird tongues. They seem to go in for plain
but wholesome foods. Won't you try the breast of
guinea hen, with a sip of Onion Soup Reine?"

"I don't care if I do," he said. "I ain't particularly
particular about what I eat."

"My nerves are all shot," I remarked airily. "New
York tires me dreadfully. I have to run about *nolens
volens*—that's Latin for willy-nilly—from one night club
to another, brushing up on old friendships. And I'm
getting so tired of shows and cocktail parties! Won't
you have a slug of hootch with me? I've got to have
one."

He gulped nervously and replied that he didn't care
if he did. I noticed with satisfaction that he was taking
in all the propaganda about night clubs, shows, and
cocktail parties.

"I'm a man of simple tastes myself," I said, lifting
both eyebrows to give my face that bored expression.
"I can't stand these silly mixed drinks. I like my liquor
straight. I'm partial to Scotch."

"I'm a rye man myself," he said. The waiter, who had
been standing by with a growingly disgusted face,

shrugged his shoulders and fetched two tiny flagons of the Old Enemy.

His face sank a little at the sight, but I managed to keep up a sophisticated front. I took a sip of soda and lifted the glass. "Well, here's looking at you and going down me."

"Corn to the corn," he said, wincing at the toast. I downed the yellow poison and so did he. I bungled the job, though, and had to use two gulps. Ooooh! I shuddered violently, but he didn't see. He had turned his face and was coughing with real fervor.

We managed to get through the meal all right, weakened though we were by the firewater. I continued to impress him. The only obstacle I hit was his reminder that I would be spending Thanksgiving on kitchen police.

We parted when I told him I couldn't get out of a reception I had to attend at 2:30. I had sufficiently impressed him and, with the aid of Providence, I might be able to borrow money from him occasionally back at Fort Bragg.

The meal cost me nothing, but the fifty-cent tip was staggering. If worst should come to worst, I could always hock my watch.

If I had a watch.

45. STOPPING IN WASHINGTON for a couple of days to mooch on the countless branches of the Hargrove family, I suddenly remembered that Ted Appelbaum was stationed at the Army War College. After trying six or eight telephone numbers, all of which gave me new numbers to call, I finally found how to reach Private Appelbaum. Except, I was told, it was now Sergeant Appelbaum.

Having known the gentle Theodore since the days when we used to cut classes together at Central High School, I knew that he would be quite proud about the sergeant's stripes. So, when I finally reached him by telephone, I said, "Don't tax your brain trying to recognize the voice, junior. This is Staff Sergeant Hargrove."

I could hear an astonished gasp at the other end of the line. "When did you get into the Army?" he roared. "And how did you get four stripes?"

"I didn't get in," I told him. "I was got. And I earned the four stripes by helping old ladies across the street."

When I finally confessed that I was still a private, he felt much better. He even invited me to come over and visit him. He even invited me to have lunch with him. At the post exchange, at that.

The War College, which, I understand, serves as general headquarters for the nation's field forces, is definitely big-time stuff. It is built on the point where the two rivers meet, and the combination of water frontage, great lawns, and stately buildings is a sight to behold.

Getting in at the front gate is a matter of some small difficulty. The Military Police at the gate knew Appelbaum and were expecting me, so I managed that part all right. From there you walk down beautiful avenues and along great green spaces to reach the college itself. When you walk up the massive front steps and into the lobby, you begin wondering if you have a foreign look or if your Piedmont drawl will be mistaken for an accent.

You are registered at the door—name, address, time of entrance into the building, and the department you wish to visit. There is a conspicuous blank left for the time of your departure. Then the guard pins a big yellow button on your lapel and you slink off toward the office where Sergeant Appelbaum is employed. The whole procedure is terrifying, to say the least, and the sight of a lieutenant general is all that would be needed to make you turn tail and flee.

After lunch, Appelbaum was permitted to have the afternoon off and we went over to see his mother, whom I hadn't seen since the three of us had dinner at Tenner's in November, 1937, the evening before Ted left to enter the Army in Hawaii.

Eve, who looks younger than her son, had eyes only for him when we entered her store. The soldier who came in with him was, to her, merely another of his constant companions. She stooped to pick a piece of paper from the floor and when she straightened up again, our eyes met. Her hand went to her mouth in astonishment.

"My God!" she said. "He's taller, and he's broader, and his clothes don't look like sleeping bags any more." From there we turned to complimenting each other.

The three of us finally wound up at a little Rumanian dining room on Thirteenth Street, where we sated ourselves on gehachte leber and enormous rib steaks and talked over all the people we knew three or four years ago. The people Ted and I went to school with at Central, the people whose iceboxes we raided on Sunday afternoons. Some of them were dead, some of them were scattered all over the country, some of them were married and surrounded by howling little bundles from heaven. Four years is a short time, but it can produce startling changes in the lives around you.

And now Appelbaum, who was once one of the worst disciplinary problems Dr. Garinger ever knew (present company excluded), was holding down a highly responsible job in the Plans and Training Department of the United States Army. He was planning to go to Aviation School to become a pilot. He was one of the finest looking soldiers you could see.

I should like to have stayed longer, but a ten-day furlough lasts only ten days. I am needed back at Fort Bragg. Like Little Orphunt Annie, I'm to wash the cups and sassers up and clear the things away.

46. THANKSGIVING DAY—with all of its roast Vermont turkey, its pies and fruits, its candles, and free cigarettes—was just another day to me. Phooey to it.

Our mess sergeant, one Orville D. Pope, was disgustingly cheerful when he awoke me in the morning. "Come, Private Hargrove," he yelled gleefully, "the Day is here! Boyoboy, are we going to give those hash hounds a holiday treat!"

"Please go away," I said. "Just go away and let me gently curse."

He was like that all morning. He bustled about the kitchen, humming idiotic little tunes while he prepared a lavish and altogether sissy meal. During all this time I stood at the sink cleaning breakfast dishes or sat in a corner peeling potatoes for dinner and supper.

"Oh, Private Hargrove," he crowed, "we have so much to be thankful for. So very, very much! We have food, and warmth, and freedom!"

"Food we've got," I growled. "Including potatoes, with peelings to peel. This is my 678th potato this morning. I don't need coal for warmth when I'm bathing myself in sweat. And freedom? See, I am laughing bitterly! It is Thanksgiving Day and I am peeling potatoes and washing dishes for the orgy. Phooey to Thanksgiving!"

Sollie Buchman, the cook who was a student with

me in Battery A, strode up humming that maudlin old grammar-school song about "over the river and through the woods, to grandfather's house we go."

"It is a glorious day," drooled Private Buchman. "It does my old heart good to think of the expressions on those boys' faces when they see that Thanksgiving dinner."

"Repress yourself, Pappy," I asked him. "It is not to think of the dinner. I am thinking of the sinks overflowing with dirty dishes left by those gluttonous hogs. It was not enough that we had trays to wash. Now we have to have improvements. Now we have to have china plates. And cups. And soup bowls. And silverware. I hate progress!"

"Better leave the lad alone, Pappy," sighed Sergeant Pope. "He is pouting and will not enter into the spirit of the day. He has done wrong and is paying for it now. He was supposed to do a Sunday KP for leaving a raincoat on his bunk all day. So he skipped out on it. Now he has to do KP on Sunday and Thanksgiving both. Do not fret yourself about him. He has a nasty attitude."

Private Buchman and the mess sergeant busied themselves at the ovens. I sat there ferociously jabbing at potatoes and muttering wildly. Three times I scowled at the sergeant, but he wasn't looking.

Maury Sher, my bosom companion from the cooks' battery, came racing in through the back door. Maury was slated to be transferred to a cook's job at Madison

Barracks, New York, and would be leaving the following day.

"If you have come to extend the season's greetings, comrade," I told him wearily, "kindly do not trouble yourself. To paraphrase Dickens, any fool who goes about with 'Happy Thanksgiving' on his lips should be boiled in his own slumgullion and buried with a GI breadstick in his heart. Do not attempt to cheer me."

"I'm not going to Madison Barracks," he shouted. "I'm staying here. Right here in the Replacement Center! I'm going to be a mess sergeant in the antitank battery. A mess sergeant!"

Sergeant Pope looked up from his work. "Did someone call me?"

"Private Sher is going to be a mess sergeant," I told him. "Private Sher will be a new type of mess sergeant, with two added qualities—a brain and a heart. Kaypees will not receive horrible treatment from HIM!"

"Back to your work," the sergeant said quietly. "I have been very lenient with you this morning. One more disrespectful word and you shall scrub the floors."

"Master Hargrove," said Sergeant-Elect Sher, "we shall continue to paint parts adjacent a pale and passionate purple. I can have my car sent down from Ohio —and when the team of Hargrove and Sher rides again, it will really ride. Listen: let's go to Charlotte the first weekend you aren't on KP and do the town up brown. And how's this for an idea—"

"Please let us exercise more dignity, Private Sher," I rebuked him. "Let us not become overly jubilant.

Let us not join in this mob of Thanksgiving sentimentalists."

Thanksgiving was just another day to me. Phooey to it.

47. YOU'VE PROBABLY NOTICED, under some pictures, the line "Photo by Bushemi." Private John A. Bushemi is official photographer for the Field Artillery Replacement Center public relations office.

Bushemi is a small, dark, pleasant looking lad of about 22. He comes from Gary, Indiana. I'd say his two chief characteristics are an unfailing energy and an unfailing sense of humor. He has a good imagination and a good sense of beauty, and he makes good pictures.

The day Bushemi came to work for our office, he was sent out with me to cover an obstacle race sponsored by the Fourth Regiment. The race was a mile-and-a-quarter affair and included climbing ladders, jumping trenches, and tunneling through pipes at the obstacle course.

Bushemi climbed a large platform, far back from the starting point, to get a picture of the start of the race. When the race started, I didn't see Bushemi's flash gun go off, so I looked around to see if he had got the picture. Bushemi jumped from the platform and whizzed by me. "Got the start," he shouted. "Now I've got to get some obstacles." And, fully equipped with camera and equipment case, Bushemi sailed off down the course behind the racers.

About six minutes later, the winner panted up to the finish ribbon. Then came the second placer, also out of breath. Then the third. Then the fourth. Then Bushemi, fresh and nonchalant.

"Sorry I didn't get back in time to take the finish," he sighed. "I guess my wind ain't as good as it once was."

When our Colonel Parker was promoted to the rank of Brigadier-General, I got the first interview, Bushemi the first picture. Bushemi photographed me interviewing the General. Then, we decided, it was only fair that I photograph Bushemi photographing the General. The picture, with all credit given to the photographic genius of Private Hargrove, appeared in the Gary *Post-Tribune*, whose staff photographer Bushemi had been before he accepted the Army's invitation.

Last week we were sent out to the firing range, where Bushemi was to take pictures of the big 155 mm. guns in action. The gun crews all scooted for cover whenever the lanyard was pulled. The terrific noise and concussion were too much for them. Bushemi, with wads of cotton waste hanging loosely from his ears, stood three feet from the huge guns and photographed every blast.

"Bushemi," I suggested, when I finally got up the courage to come out of my retreat far behind the firing line, "this is too good to waste. Suppose I take a picture of you taking a picture of the gunfire. The Gary paper would eat that up."

So I did. Bushemi focused the spare camera and set all the adjustments. Apart from the fact that I almost fell over backwards when the gun fired, I did fairly well. Bushemi said that he would teach me photography.

When we got back to the office and printed the pictures, there was some little amusement. This was getting to be a deadly routine, the office force decided. Hargrove taking a picture of Bushemi taking a picture of something.

"Man," said Bushemi, "if you think that's good, just wait until we get another photographer. His only job will be taking pictures of Hargrove taking pictures of Bushemi taking pictures of the original photographer taking pictures of Hargrove. That is, until the Captain decides to get an entire new staff."

48. I WAS DAWDLING OVER A HUGE chocolate nut sundae the other night at the Service Club cafeteria when Johnny Lisk walked in with someone who was a dead ringer for Simmons Jones of the Charlotte *News* staff. Anyone who is a dead ringer for Simmons Jones can't be anybody but Simmons Jones, I decided, so I gave the low whistle. The two saw me and came over.

It was Simmons, all right. He looked as if the two things he needed most at the moment were a haircut and a kind word of sympathy. He had the look of utter futility known only to those who have been in the Army for less than ten days. Poor Simmons was in bad shape.

"Well, boy," I asked him, "how do you like the Army? And you don't need to lie about it."

"I don't think I'll ever get used to it," he said. "I've been pushed and crowded and yelled at for a week now, and it doesn't get any better. Maybe I was just born to be a civilian."

"You should have seen Johnny and me when we got in," I told him. "That's been only four months ago, and here we are being condescending and fatherly already. Them were the days, weren't they, Johnny?"

Lisk sighed deeply. "Simmons don't know trouble at all," he said. "When Hargrove and I had been in three or four days, they slapped us on KP and almost killed us first thing. Then, the next day, they put the two of us to cleaning and painting GI cans until past supper-time."

Simmons knocked on wood. "Well, they must have forgotten me. I've been in the Army a week already and I haven't been on KP yet."

"You will, brother," said Johnny. "You will."

"Hargrove," said Simmons, "will you please stop looking at my hair? I can't go ten feet without being reminded to get a haircut. As soon as I can find a minute, I'll get it cut."

"Are you really having a hard time of it?" I asked him.

"Well, after that talk I got from you before I was inducted, I thought I would be going through hell for the first three weeks. The way you talked was terrifying, to say the least. So I prepared myself for a much rougher time than I'm really getting.

"The drilling isn't bad at all. I suppose my dancing has helped me there. Anyway, I even surprise myself at it.

"But the getting up and dressing in ten minutes! I'll never be able to do it. Everything is all right until it comes to the leggins. I struggle with those things until I'm limp, and I never do get them on in time. Yesterday I just tied them on for reveille and sneaked back and put them on properly later. I've tried every way possible, but I just can't get anywhere with them."

"How are the fellows?" I asked him. "Nice bunch of boys?"

"I was surprised at them," he said. "People I've never

seen before, and they all go out of their way to help each other. When we were first inducted, there were a lot of fellows I'd seen possibly once or twice before in my life and we all acted as if we'd known each other since we were babies.

"Then, too, I've already run across some of the boys I know. Johnny here is attached to our battery for rations and quarters, and so is Buster Charnley. They do as much as they can to show me the ropes and help me along during this awkward period."

"Well, Simmons," Johnny said, "it's like they told you before you came in. The Army will certainly make a man of you. Look at Hargrove there. He'd never done a good day's work in his life before he got into the Army. Now he's the potato-peeling champion of five regiments."

"Private Lisk," I said coldly, "let us not bring personalities into this."

Fortunately, Miss Scarborough, senior hostess of the Service Club, passed by and I was able to yank her into the company. The discussion was avoided.

49. READING THROUGH THE CAMP NEWS-PAPER the other day, I noticed stories written by Pvt. T. Mulvehill, Private Thos. Mulvehille, Pfc. Tom

Mulvehill, Thomas Mulvehill (pfc.), and various other authors whose names bore startling resemblance to Thomas Mulvehill, Pvt. or Pfc.

The collection of literary and journalistic contributions to the Fort Bragg *Post* were all marked by the same flair for rhetoric, the true gift of gab, and a certain rich and gorgeous sentimentality. In the midst of a factual story about a group of college girl choristers coming to Fort Bragg for a concert, the steady journalistic strain would suddenly burst into brilliant and majestic phrases such as "The Blankth Battalion recreation hall will burst into golden sound next Tuesday night when the angelic voices of thirty lovely Zilch College young ladies present a recital . . ." or "the General's little eight-year-old son, awed by the solemnity of the occasion, clung to his daddy's hand throughout the impressive ceremonies."

This is what is known as the Mulvehill Touch.

The Mulvehill Touch is supplied at Fort Bragg by the Public Relations Office's irrepressible and inimitable whirling dervish, Black Tom Mulvehill, a fantastic and unbelievable Irish tyro, who came from New York City by way of Salt Lake City, Utah. Mulvehill of the great head and the shaggy locks, Mulvehill of the lumbering walk, the man of a thousand faces and a thousand voices—Mulvehill is the Public Relations Office's one spark of true glamour, our one hope of immortality.

Mulvehill is everywhere at all times. Out of every hundred photographs taken at Fort Bragg—official or personal, professional or amateur—it is safe to say that the flexible face of Private Mulvehill will beam out at you from ninety-five of them. Photographers have no idea of how he gets into the pictures, but a picture of any "Rec" hall in the Center will show Mulvehill playing ping-pong. (He's the one nearest the camera.)

A photograph of a dance—any dance—will show Mulvehill grinning at the lens. A series of recreational pictures taken any Saturday night will show Black Tom at a soldiers' dance in Raleigh; at the Soldier's Town Home in Fayetteville, fully sixty miles away; Black Tom, wearing scholarly glasses, singing in a chapel choir; Lieuthomas Mulvehill reading in the Service Club library; Mulvehill drinking beer in at least four different post exchanges.

This is no prearranged idea of the photographers; they are helpless before his ability to be everywhere at once and in every picture they take. It is the will of Allah.

Mulvehill's next greatest talent is his ability to create wildness and confusion at will. His desk drawers bulge and spill great quantities of unrelated papers, old notes, newspaper clippings, and weird personal effects. His working schedule and methods are chaotic and unfathomable. He can write six stories at once, using every needed typewriter in the building.

The Lieuthomas is now engaged in a great and bitter feud with the mess sergeant. The sergeant, a comparatively new man at the job, is extremely anxious to give his mess hall a clean, quiet, and clublike atmosphere—a place of charm and beauty. An entire lovely meal is spoiled for him when the mellow voice of Mulvehill roars above the gentle hum of the room, in an extemporaneous take-off on the March of Time, a hilarious Jewish protest against some injustice of the morning, or a smooth Greek-accented request for "joost wan slicea brad, pliz."

The mess sergeant's repeated pleas for dignity and decorum meet with little co-operation from the whirling dervish. Mulvehill merely bends his huge body almost level with his waist, turns his head almost to the back of his neck, looks sweetly up into the mess sergeant's face and tenderly asks, "Whatsa trobble from you, pliz, pal?" The mess sergeant groans wearily and retreats in disorder.

That one name—the immortal name of Thos. Mulvehill, Pfc.—makes sergeants wail, Service Club hostesses sigh with futility, and the public relations officer wish sometimes that he were in the parachute troops.

That boy Mulvehill!

50. I'M STILL NOT THE EXECUTIVE TYPE, I suppose. People to the right and left of me, fellows who were selected with me last July, pass on up the

ladder while I sit here in the sunshine and watch. But they also serve who only stand and wait.

Take Big Jim Hart and Fred McPhail. Jim and I went to Central together (on the days I was there) and I even acted as his campaign manager the time we lost the election for treasurer of the student council. Jim stood with *News* State Editor Willie Weisner and me in front of the Armory one chilly morning last July, waiting for the sunrise and the medical examiners. Fred was our bus leader the morning we stood in front of the bus station, waiting for Draft Board Number Five and whatever fate awaited us. They were both assigned to the antitank battery when I had cooking chosen as my true art.

Both of them dropped in this evening for a neighborly call.

Having finished learning the basic lessons in how to fight off an unruly tank, they were chosen by their battery, battalion and regimental commanders as bright boys with possibilities and their names were submitted to a special board of officers as good material for the FARC (Field Artillery Replacement Center) School, composed of outstanding selectees from all over the Center. From a large list of candidates for the school, they were chosen by the board to attend the school with a small group of selectees from other organizations in the Center.

Now they are going through a rigorous but valuable month's course in administration, dismounted drill, communication, instrument and firing data, firing battery, military courtesy, gunnery, hygiene and sanitation, motor maintenance, rifle marksmanship, chemical warfare, mess management, military law, and an imposing list of other equally terrifying subjects.

Out of their class, a small number—I think it's about twenty-six—will be chosen as candidates for admission to the Officers' Candidate School at Fort Sill, Oklahoma. The pick of the class at Sill will be commissioned as officers in the Army of the United States.

If Fred and Jim make the grade here—and they have one chance out of three—they will be officially recommended here as officer candidates. If they don't make it, they will serve as highly trained noncommissioned officers. Either way, they've been highly honored before they've been in the Army five months.

While Fred and Jim were still here, Maury Sher and Whitey Grafenstein came in, smoking tailor-made cigarettes and beaming prosperously. Both of them were in the old student cooks' battery with me. Maury is my severest friend and best critic. I try to borrow money from him and, without even asking what I want it for, he refuses the loan. He is free with his cigarettes, though, and you can't expect a man to be perfect. Whitey is a strong and silent Wisconsin lad who shared many hardships with me in the struggle to master the arts of the kitchen.

Now Maury is mess sergeant in the same antitank battery which trained so many Charlotte boys of our cycle—the battery where McPhail and Hart are stationed—and Grafenstein is a cook in the battery next door.

"Well, old one," said Sergeant Sher, "look at them two boys. Don't they look well-fed and healthy?"

"Positively bloated," I said, reaching for his cigarettes. "What are you feeding them now—dried apples and water?"

The two old friends from Charlotte, turncoats that they are, rose to defend the food put out by the new mess sergeant. It seems that Sher, an old restaurateur (two to one, the linotypers will put an 'n' in that word) from Columbus, Ohio, has great plans for the kitchen of Battery D, Third Battalion. Before he had been there for three days, he shanghied Grafenstein from next door and worked half the night baking pies for the next day. Now he is working on a scheme to get Grafenstein transferred to his kitchen, where he will keep the poor boy up seven nights a week at the same job.

Ah, they're doing well, these boys. Going through special training, lording it over their own kitchens and a' that. Yessir, they're doing well.

It's good for me that I'm not ambitious. Once a private, always a private—that's me.

51. ORVILLE D. POPE, MESS SERGEANT of Head-quarters Battery and master of all he surveys (so long as he stays in the kitchen), strolled past our table like a happy night-club owner inspecting his saloon.

Bushemi lifted a forkful of creamed potatoes to his mouth, made a sour face and inserted the potatoes as if they were seasoned with liniment. Don Bishop, the public relations reporter who sometimes shows a streak of sheer sanity, lifted his coffee, held his nose and drank it.

"Sergeant Pope," I said in a small voice, "earlier in the course of this supper I told you that I had never tasted anything harder or drier than the bread you served us tonight. I want to take that back, Pope. When I said that, I hadn't tasted your peanut butter."

Sergeant Pope paused and gazed at us with heavy disgust. "The gentlemen of the press," he said. "There ought to be something in the Articles of War about letting guys like you into a respectable mess hall."

"Then after they wrote that Article of War," said Bishop, "they could put in an amendment about letting us in mess halls like this one of yours."

"Some chow you're putting out these days, Pope," said Bushemi. "Like nothing I ever ate—unfortunately! What are you doing—saving money to get married?"

"You're the only ones I ever hear griping about the chow in this battery," said Pope. "You're the only ones

I ever have trouble with. You three and Mulvehill. If I'll pay for your food, won't you please take all your meals at the Service Club?"

"Let's leave Mulvehill's name out of this," I said. "Poor, poor old Mulvehill. We knew him well. He was a good boy, was the Lieuthomas."

"I noticed the place is so quiet tonight that you can even hear Bushemi eating his celery," said the sergeant. "Where is your dear friend Mulvehill, the bum?"

"You have run him over the hill," said Bishop. "Your food and your mess hall and your brutishly foul mouth have driven him away. He has deserted from the Army and his guilt is upon your hands."

Before the sergeant could ask further into Mulvehill's absence, Bishop deftly turned the subject. "Right after lunch today, I went over to the Service Club to get something to eat and who do you suppose I saw there?"

"You saw Miss Harden, the hostess of the Ninth Division," said Bushemi. "And you told us about it as soon as you got to the office. You know the one thing that's missing from this meal—the one thing that would make it perfect?"

"Ice cream?" asked the mess sergeant.

"Chloroform," said Bushemi.

Pope slapped his forehead mightily. "Why couldn't I have been a dud-picker, a horse valet, a suicide submarineman—anything but a mess sergeant? Where is Mulvehill?" He wrinkled his forehead. "Say! He wasn't here at breakfast either."

"Nor lunch," said Bishop. "Nor supper, nor lunch, nor breakfast yesterday."

"He has gone over the hill," I said, gloomily. "He has deserted."

Before the sergeant could press the question further, Bushemi started up the talk anew. "I've got to get a haircut," he said. "Should I get a GI haircut or just run a lawn mower over my head? The lawn mower does a prettier job."

"Why don't you just burn off the brush?" I asked him. "That's the cheapest way."

"Let's see," said the sergeant. "He wasn't here all day today and he didn't come in yesterday and he didn't show up for supper the night before last. Is he sick?"

"He would have been," said Bishop, "if he hadn't got a decent meal soon."

"I can remember Mulvehill just like he was right here with us even now," I said. "He was a fine, noble, sensitive lad. He had a beautiful career before him in the Army. Fate can ruin any of us by tossing in the tiniest little monkey wrench—or the toughest little biscuit. I hated to see Mulvehill go over the hill."

"Cut the clowning," the sergeant wailed, convinced at last that Mulvehill had flown. "You can't make me think that he left because of my food. Where is he?"

"That," sighed Bishop, "is what the War Department would like to know."

Pope began drumming unconsciously on the table. "I know my food is as good as any in the Center. That ain't it. Did he take offense at something I said to him and start eating at the Service Club?"

Acton Dennington Hawkins the Third, chief cook, passed by. "Where's your friend Mulvehill?" he asked us.

"Oh," said Bushemi, forgetting the play, "Mulvehill's on furlough."

The mess sergeant rose with a roar. "The day shall come!" he screamed. "You'll all be on KP one of these days! Oh, will you suffer and will I enjoy myself! Finish your supper and get out of my mess hall! Get out! GET OUT!"

We got.

52. "AS IF I DIDN'T HAVE ENOUGH TROUBLE on my hands with payday," said Top Sergeant Tate, "now I have to be exposed to the sight of you. Be brief."

"Sergeant," I began, "when I hear people say a soldier can't live on the pay he makes, I'd like to show them myself as a living proof that he can."

"Quit beating your gums," he said, "and get to the point. You didn't come in here to compliment the Army on its pay. And take your cap off when you're in the orderly room."

"I didn't come to compliment nobody nor nothing," I said, laying my cap on the corner of his desk. "I just came in to see if the War Department is mad at me. They haven't given me a cent of salary since the first of October."

"What in the sweet name of heaven are you talking about?" the top kick hooted, handing me back the cap. "We've had two regular paydays, including the one today. And we've had two supplementary payrolls for people who missed the regular paydays."

"Mind you," I put in, "I'm not complaining. I eat regularly and I have a roof over my head. I can get haircuts and movie tickets and cigarettes and shoe polish on credit, but I certainly would like a little cash spending money from time to time."

"Well," he groaned, slapping his desk wearily, "here we go again, Hargrove, the boy who makes a top kick's life exciting! Hargrove the hopeless—the sloppy bunk on inspection day, the soap in the soup, the thorn in the side. Hargrove, the boy who can take the simplest problem and reduce it to its most confusing form. Now let's start at the beginning and take the whole thing slowly. You haven't been paid since October first. How come?"

"That was because when the November first payday came around, I had just got here. I signed the October payroll in my old battery."

"All right," he said patiently, counting off a finger. "That's one payday. That brings us up to November tenth, the day of the supplementary payroll, when you should have got the pay you missed on the first. Did you sign the supplementary payroll for that occasion?"

"Yes, sir," I insisted. "Then when the supplementary payday came around, something happened. Or to be more correct, nothing happened. I still didn't get paid."

"That's two paydays you missed," the sergeant sighed. "I will check into the second later. Now—what about today's pay?"

"I missed out on that one too. The battery commander couldn't find my signature on the payroll."

"Isn't that just too utterly delightful?" he cooed. "Couldn't find your signature on the payroll! You know, I'll bet some nasty old thing came along with ink eradicator and erased your signature from it! If your signature wasn't on the payroll, Private Hargrove, it was because you hadn't signed the payroll!"

"That makes sense," I conceded.

He patted me on both shoulders, a little heavily, and I cowered. "Wait just a minute, Private Hargrove," he said sweetly. "Let sargie-wargie see what he can find out about the nasty old payroll."

He returned in a few minutes, frowning wearily. "Private Hargrove," he sighed, "dear Private Hargrove! You didn't draw your pay on the tenth of November because you weren't here on the tenth! You were on furlough! And you didn't sign the payroll for today because you were on furlough while it was being signed. Your modest pay for October has been in the battery safe for three weeks, just waiting for you to get around to picking it up!"

He took a small envelope from behind his back. "Twenty-one dollars for services rendered through the month of October. Harrumph! Minus two-forty for theater tickets, minus a dollar for haircuts, minus seven dollars for canteen checks. Private Hargrove, I present to you your October wages—ten dollars and sixty cents!"

I took the money, looked at it tenderly, and crammed it into my pocket.

"And Private Hargrove," said the top kick, "in a few days you will see a notice on the bulletin board asking all men who were not paid today to come in and sign the supplementary payroll. When you see that notice, Private Hargrove, I want you to come right into the orderly room so I can explain it to you. Then I want to watch you while you sign the payroll, so that we'll be sure to get it right. Will you do that much for your old top sergeant?"

"Yes, sir," I promised. "May I go now, sergeant?"

"Yes, Private Hargrove," he sighed. "Please do."

53. WINTER, AT LAST, IS UPON US. In the rear ranks, the surest indication is to be found in reveille.

All through the late summer and the fall, we hopped out of bed as soon as the whistle blew. Now we crawl grumblingly out when the sergeant puts the whistle to his lips for a "Fall out!" blast. Since it is still dark when we stand reveille, and since we are aided occasionally by a heaven-sent fog, there are many saviors of democracy who slip on merely a pair of shoes (partially laced), a pair of trousers, and a field jacket. The field jacket, when buttoned all the way to the collar, hides the absence of shirt and tie—and the sergeant is none the wiser.

In Headquarters Battery, the process of getting up in the morning has sunk into a rut of repetition. It's the same procedure every morning.

Sergeant Roughton, platoon leader, toots his brass at six o'clock and a few energetic soldiers at the other end of the squadroom rise and begin the morning with sickeningly cheerful horseplay. They yank the covers off their neighbors. The neighbors yank the covers back on.

Private First Class Bishop, unofficial guardian of the public relations staff, rises from his bunk which is next to mine. "Hargrove! Bushemi! Get up! Salute the morn!" Then he yells down the length of the squadroom to the bed of Private First Class Thomas ("Thoss") Mulvehill.

Mulvehill, every morning, has already been forcibly ejected from his bed by his wild neighbors. He is, by this time, sitting on the edge of his bunk, with his great head sunk between his knees and his fingers fumbling with his shoelaces. In a thick and fiery Irish brogue, he is berating whatever forces of destiny put him in this mad corner of the squadroom.

I stick a cautious toe out from under the covers. The outer air isn't cold but, then again, it isn't warm. I roll over and look at the next bunk, where Private Bushemi is snoring gently. I roll back, get comfortable, and pull the cover over my head.

"Hargrove!" roars Bishop. "Get your lazy bones out of bed! It's five after six!"

"Call me at ten after six," I mutter. "Better still just sing out when my name is called at reveille."

Private Bishop reaches over suddenly and rips the blankets from the bunk. I rise, cursing him soundly. Private Bushemi is still sleeping, with a sweet and childish smile on his face. I lift a foot and give him a firm shove in the posterior.

"Git out of there, you blankety-blanked dash-dash, shiftless, good-for-nothing bum!" I shout, giving him two or three more shoves. "Git out of there or I'll dump you out!"

"Do me a favor, Hargrove," he growls. "Crawl off somewhere and die. Just one more time you're going to raise that club foot of yours and I'm going to get up and clip you one. Now go away."

I reach over and grab the edge of Bushemi's bunk. I joggle it slightly to give the impression that I am just about to overturn the bunk. Bushemi bounces out of bed, swinging wildly. "You're going to get funny just one morning too often, and I'm going to beat the eternal perdition out of both of you. It's getting to the point where it ain't funny." Then he begins mumbling aimlessly under his breath as he steps into his trousers.

Somehow, we manage to get into the second shoe just as the whistle blows to call us outside. We shiver in the dark cold as section leaders call the roll, mostly from memory. The second section of the first platoon is always the last to finish roll call. We stand there listening. "P-o-g-g-i!" "Hyoh!" "Pulver!" "Here!" and then the pièce de résistance: "Peacock!" Always the answer comes in the same way—an unbelievably deep bass, long-drawn-out and rumbling: "Heeeeeeere!" The second platoon snickers and titters, just as it did the day before, and the top kick shouts, "Dismissed!"

Bushemi heads straight back for his bunk. "Call me at chowtime, will you?"

Breakfast time arrives and again we begin the ordeal of getting Bushemi up. He lies there, fully clothed by this time, with a blanket thrown over him. "Call me at seven-fifteen, will you?" After swearing not to lend him money for coffee at the Service Club on his way to work, we strike out for the mess hall.

The morning has begun.

54. BILL, A FRIEND OF BUSHEMI'S and mine in Charlotte, drives a street bus. Before he began his service as a driver, he served a hitch in the Army. Like all ex-service men, he's ready to drop everything and

just shoot the breeze any time the conversation turns to the Army.

I like to listen to them, these old soldiers. All of them have, at one time or another, been standing at attention during retreat and had a gnat land on the nose. They describe with graphic language the way those little cusses hang on to your nose, no matter how much you blow at them from the corner of your mouth.

They'll remember, too, such little details as the sweat that drips from under your cap and into your eyes while you stand inspection on a sultry summer day, and the fact that every time you try to push your cap a little to the side with your rifle when you shift to "right shoulder arms," the rifle knocks your cap all the way off your head and there's the lieutenant, asking you to step out of ranks.

Or, "Private Blank, what have you got in your mouth?" And the answer, "Gulp. Nothing, sir!"

But to get back to Bill, the bus driver.

"There was a young first-class private got on my bus last week," he told me, "and he sat in the long seat behind me, so we got started talking. Well, I thought I'd snow him under, telling him about the time I was in the Army. So, just to start the ball rolling and get the talk turned to the Army, I asked him how long he'd been in.

" 'Oh, I've been in for well over eight months,' he said, like he was just starting his thirtieth year of service. Then he started wiping his sleeves so I'd be sure to notice his private-first-class stripe.

"I thought I'd let him blow off about his stripe, so I asked him, 'Say, what does that stripe stand for?'

" 'Oh, that,' he said, as much as to say aw-shucks-that-ain't-nothing. 'That just means I'm a sergeant.'

" 'Is that right?' I asked him, looking sort of wide-mouthed at him.

" 'Yessir,' he said, real casual, 'in the Army only eight months and I've already been made sergeant.'

" 'Well, tell me,' I said, 'what grade of sergeant are you? I've seen some sergeants have three stripes and then I've seen them have as many as six. How come that?'

" 'Well,' he said, hemming and hawing a little, 'three stripes means he's just a plain buck sergeant. Six stripes is a master sergeant. I'm a supply sergeant. That's two grades above a buck sergeant and one grade below a master sergeant. I'm expecting to be a master sergeant in a month or so. That's as high as you can get.'

"I didn't say anything for a while; just sat there looking like I was letting it soak in. Then I asked him, real calm-like and ignorant, 'How many stripes does a private first class have?'

"So help me, he looked like he was going to choke for a while. Then he came back with a snappy answer in a flash.

" 'Well,' he said, 'first-class privates have one stripe, just like us supply sergeants, only their stripe is bottom-upward from ours. Their stripes point down.'

"Well, sir, I thought I'd die. I almost popped trying to keep from laughing, but I kept a straight face. Then

I said, 'Things sure have changed since I was in the Army. Back then, three or four years ago, supply sergeants were just plain buck sergeants and first-class privates were the only one-stripe men.'

" 'Yeah,' he said, sort of weak-like, 'time changes a lot of things.'

"That was all he had to say. He looked sort of foolish and pulled the cord to get off at the next stop.

"So there was another bull session shot to hell. Maybe it was for the best, though. I didn't have a chance against a fellow with that much talent."

55. I RAN OUT OF CIGARETTES this afternoon near my old cooks' battery, so I thought I'd drop in on First Sergeant Goldsmith, who smokes the same brand that I do. Sergeant Goldsmith is the old type of top sergeant, with a heart of GI shoe leather and a voice that would put the stoutest bugle to shame.

"Great gods and little paychecks," he railed. "Look what's loose again! What's the latest, little man, or aren't reporters supposed to know?"

"The only news I've heard today," I told him, helping myself to a coffin nail from his desk, "is that they're sending all the first sergeants in the Replacement Center to Panama for hard-labor service detachments.

Polish your brass and you might make acting corporal before the war's over."

Oh, it's lovely to run into an old top sergeant who can't put you on kitchen police when you sass back at him.

"Well, son," said Goldie, "any time they need an instructor in coal hauling or fertilizer pitching, I'll write out a recommendation for you. We were going to give you a specialist's rating in cavalry sanitation before you left us."

"You haven't got a light, have you?" I asked, taking the lighted cigarette from his hand. I dumped three more fags from his pack into my hand and stuffed them into my shirt pocket. "Our photographer smokes too," I explained.

"The first sergeant over in your battery tells me," he said, "that you spend so much time on KP that the boys all think you're the mess sergeant."

"How are things over here," I asked him, "now that I've left and you have to get somebody else to do your reading and writing?"

"You're a sweet little lad, Hargrove," he purred. "We really do miss you here. When you were here, I never had to worry about where I was going to get another man when there was a stovepipe to be cleaned or a street to be swept. Now I have to go and search around—search, mind you—for someone who's been a bad little boy. Never had that trouble when you were here."

"Sergeant," I told him, propping my feet on his

wastebasket, "you never miss the water until it's gone under the bridge. This battery owes a lot to me. Look out there at that grass growing in front of the orderly room. That grass wouldn't even be there—much less be that green—if I hadn't spent time and labor sprinkling it with fertilizer. And think how much cleaner the windows were when I was here to wash every one of them every week. I'll bet you haven't had a clean floor in the battery since I laid down my mop."

"Yessir," he said, "you sure were a comfort. It meant a lot to me to know when I came to work in the morning that I'd find you there, smiling at me from the sickbook, telling me that you had a pain in the belly and didn't feel like working today.

"Yessir, Hargrove," he sighed, "we sure would like to have you back in the battery again." He looked at my feet, laid carelessly across his wastebasket. "Yessir," he said, "I'd sure like to be your top sergeant again, if only for a day."

"How's Sergeant Ooton making out with his grocery budget?" I asked. "Trying to feed you on forty-two cents a day? The last time I saw him, he was working out plans to feed you on Buncombe County turnip greens or pay you to eat at the Service Club."

"Oh, that," he said. "I've saved so much on cigarettes since you left the battery that I could afford to eat uptown now if I wanted to. And let's leave any snide remarks about Buncombe County out of this. And let's leave your feet out of my wastebasket."

We sat for a while in silence and then he looked out

the window, where a yardbird in blue denims pushed a stable broom across the battery street. "Yessir, Hargrove," he said, "I sure would like to have you back in my battery."

"You're a good first sergeant, Goldie," I told him, "if you can use the words 'good' and 'first sergeant' in the same sentence. But you're getting old. Why don't you retire?" I rose to leave and he picked up his package of cigarettes before I could reach it.

"Say hello to your top sergeant," he said. "He and I are old friends. Tell him I'm planning to pay him a visit soon. There's something I want to talk over with him.

"There's one thing about top sergeants, Hargrove," he said, rubbing his hands. "They always stick together."

It looks like a long, hard winter.

56. FROM NOW ON I MUST DENY MYSELF one of the fundamental rights and joys of mankind. I must quit bumming matches from those near and dear to me —that is, if I want them to remain near and dear to me. Whenever I ask anyone around Center Headquarters— even Mulvehill or Bishop or Bushemi—for a match, I get one of two answers, both of which are getting very

tiresome by now. I hear either "What's the matter? Has your fire gone out?" or "Just light your cigarette on one of our conflagrations; there should be a small arson in yonder corner."

Since I am a patient and long-suffering child, I make no scathing remarks in return for these jaded witticisms. I merely shrug my frail shoulders pathetically and seek greener pastures. It isn't so bad, their refusing the match. The worst part of it is the reminder of an incident which might well be forgotten. The incident is of no consequence, but it might as well come off my chest.

Being a slave to that despoiler of human health and well-being, the cigarette, I still have a fondness for an occasional switch to a pipe. I don't especially enjoy the taste of pipe tobacco, and I don't believe even the most avid pipe smoker especially cares for it. Most of them, like me, merely like the feel of a pipe in their mouths and the dignity and solemnity a pipe gives them when they punctuate their conversations by jabbing the air with it.

Smoking a pipe only occasionally, I still have not become overly proficient at keeping the little things burning. When I buy a can of pipe tobacco, I buy a five-cent box of country matches with it. Half my smoke is tobacco; the other half is Georgia pine smoke from the matchsticks.

I was busy today typing out a story, and I had lit my pipe for about the twenty-second time. I threw the match into the wastebasket and forgot all about the whole thing. I was absorbed in my work.

I noticed by degrees that our office was becoming lighter and warmer. I noted the fact with a rich feeling of comfort, but no great interest in finding out the cause. It wasn't until I reached for another match to light that pipe again that I noticed my wastebasket. The thing had in it a cheerful little blaze bright enough to take action photographs on a moonless night.

There was nothing to get excited about, I told the remainder of the public relations staff, the sergeant major's corps of assistants, and the filing department. I nonchalantly put my foot into the basket and started stamping the fire out. The thing would have worked, too, except that the length of my foot was greater than the diameter of the wastebasket. The foot stuck and I could not stomp.

Corporal Sager, of Plans and Training, leaped to the rescue, pried the foot from the basket, grabbed the basket and sped away to the water cooler. I followed him and poured myself a cup of water. I still saw no cause for excitement.

To the bystanders' catcalls, unseemly laughter, and accusations of arson, I turned a fatherly ear and a quieting voice. I explained patiently that setting fire to wastebaskets was an ancient and honored pastime in the newspaper world. I told them that one of the best newspapermen North Carolina has ever seen—"Uncle John" Dickson, former city editor of the *News*—used to set his wastebasket on fire at least twice a week by tossing cigarettes or burning matches into it. It was a mark of certain industry, a sign that a man was wrapped up in his work.

Nevertheless, the incident has established for me a new reputation of carelessness and absent-mindedness, one which I do not deserve. I shall be hooted at from the windows of the Service Club; even green rookies will snicker when I dodder down Headquarters Street.

It does no good to point out Bushemi, who often walks out of the mess hall with his dirty dishes in his hands, or Mulvehill, who puts new blades in his razor without removing the old ones and thereby gives his face the old bacon-slicer treatment. Nothing does any good. Whenever I try to defend myself, I get deeper in the mess.

Idleness and soft living have made my comrades a bunch of drawing-room hecklers. Boy, wouldn't I like to get these babies out on maneuvers with me!

57. MULVEHILL WENT OVER TO THE POST OFFICE the other day to get a story on the big business handled there during the holidays. He came back with this story, which he swears he saw happen before his very eyes:

A young soldier walked up to the mailing window

and slapped a loosely wrapped package on the counter. When the package landed, there was that lovely clanking sound that comes only when two glass objects meet each other.

The clerk examined the package and found that it contained a number of bottles of perfume, placed there with no kind of packing between them. They had been dumped carelessly into the box and allowed to jostle about and bounce off each other.

"I'm sorry, soldier," the clerk said, "but we can't accept this for mailing."

"You can't?" The boy was astonished. "How come you can't?"

"Well," said the clerk, "the way it's wrapped, it would break before it got where it was going."

"Oh, that's all right," said the soldier. "I'm going to insure it."

One of the worst problems that faces the post office here at the Replacement Center is the religious attention the new recruits give to all orders and directions. This is all very well and good, but all men are told to execute orders intelligently rather than obey them blindly.

One of the first things a new recruit sees when he gets here is a sample mailing address, to show him how to show his friends and neighbors how to address their mail to him.

The sample address usually reads "Pvt. John Doe, Battery A, Eleventh Battalion, Fourth Training Regiment, Field Artillery, Replacement Center, Fort Bragg, N. C."

You may say that I am lying; you may say that I am trying to be funny. But I swear that this is the truth. Every time a new training cycle begins, the FARC post office is swamped with letters addressed to "Private John Doe," with whatever battery address the sample states.

The Message Center which deals with all telegrams and all communications within the Center, has its little problems too. Last week it received one of those pretty Christmas telegrams addressed to "Private John Goodow, New Recruit, Fort Bragg, N. C."

There's another little story which started with Private Warnke, the Brooklyn brain trust over in the classification office. Private Warnke reports that one of the colored selectees here was being questioned by one of the officers about his work.

The boy worked, he said, on "one of them big guns."

Since practically everybody in Field Artillery Center works on one of them big guns, the answer was considered vague.

"Just what do you do on them big guns?" the officer asked him.

"Oh, I'm the do'man," the soldier replied.

"I've been an officer in the artillery for longer than I can remember," the officer said, "and I've never heard of an artillery piece having a do'man. What do you do in your work as a do'man?"

"Well, sir," the boy explained, "I opens the do' on

them big guns and then somebody slides a shell in. Then I closes the do'."

The explanation sufficed to show that the young man was the number-one man on a 155-millimeter howitzer!

There are untold numbers of good stories—at least, better than these—that I could tell if I weren't honor bound to stick to the truth.

58. PRIVATE JOHN A. ("ONE-SHOT") BUSHEMI, official FARC photographer, has added another laurel to his stack. His photograph of a young soldier standing on a hilltop is on the cover of the January issue of the *Field Artillery Journal,* which is a national honor.

Personally, I am getting quite fed up with this Bushemi.

Money could not pay for the things I have done for that boy. Every morning for months I have awakened him and dragged him out of bed so that he would not be absent from reveille. I have lugged his laundry from the supply room when I went to get my own. I have given to him freely my hard-mooched cigarettes. I have toted his heavy equipment case from one end of Fort Bragg to the other a thousand times. But does he have gratitude? He does not.

Bushemi is like the camel in the old proverb. This

camel, whom we will call Bushemi, stuck his head into his master's tent one cold night and asked permission to keep it there. That granted, he next asked permission to bring his front shoulders into the tent. This kept up until the camel was inside the tent and the poor man was shivering outside in just his nightie.

Several weeks ago, I brought Bushemi over to Charlotte to meet the *News'* managing editor and to date the girl friend of my girl friend. The next week he took me over to Charlotte.

Within a week of the time he first entered Charlotte, he had completely taken over the town. His roguish eye and his sickening line of bull had completely overwhelmed the poor girl to whom he was presented. When we entered the *News* office together, everybody greeted Bushemi with a hearty hand and me with a casual nod. He worked his cunning wiles over his new girl friend's family and neatly had himself adopted by them from the start.

It was bad enough when he began inviting me to go to Charlotte with him over the weekend, but when he started being solicitous about my comfort, that was too much. "Poor, lonely, neglected little Hargrove," he would say with disgusting tenderness, "doesn't anybody love you? If you haven't got a date for tonight, I can fix you up with the cutest little brunette you ever cast an eye on."

That was the last straw. Poor, lonely, neglected little Hargrove! Bushemi, Private Bushemi of Fort Bragg and Charlotte, would fix me up if I couldn't get a date!

"Private Bushemi," I reminded him coldly on several occasions, "please be so good as to remember that this is *my* home town, that I have my own friends here even if I don't have a family here, and that I am quite capable of taking care of myself—of arranging my own dates—without the help of a half-pint Hoosier cameraman. Please go away; you nauseate me."

But I knew, even when I said them, that my words were empty and without conviction. I knew that I had been the victim of a false and crafty charlatan, a smooth slicker from the Yankee Northland. I had been crowded out of Charlotte.

"You look hungry, little Hargrove," he would purr on Sunday afternoon. "Come and have a good meal with the little woman and me." And the Little Woman would beam approvingly at her Johnny's thoughtfulness.

Before the thing had gone on very long, it swooped to the climax. I took my eyes for a few moments off the little creature who furnished the chief incentive for my sneaking to Charlotte whenever I could. When I looked at her again, she was sitting across the room, with her hand in the hand of this cunning Eye-talian and her eyes looking up into his.

There is no need for me to visit Charlotte again. There is nothing left there for me. It's Bushemi territory. If I ever get a furlough again, I'll probably have to go to Gary, Indiana.

59. THE REPLACEMENT CENTER'S BITTER-EST and most beloved feud came to a head Sunday. The principals are Private First Class (Specialist Second Class) Charlie Warnke, known as the Brooklyn Eagle, and Private First Class (Specialist Third Class) Acton Dennington Hawkins the Third, chief cook of Headquarters Battery.

It was a bad day for the Eagle.

The Eagle and several of his cronies were returning from their Christmas furloughs in New York when they ran into the back end of a convoy which the Eagle swears had three thousand troop trucks in it. The three thousand trucks, which they refused to leapfrog, slowed them up to such an extent that the party returned to the battery the day after they were supposed to get back.

The first sergeant was impressed with the story of the troop convoy and was quite sympathetic toward the three tardy men. He could not understand, however, how they were restrained from sending him a telegram to keep him from worrying about their safety. The first sergeant was quite cut up about their thoughtlessness in the matter. So the first sergeant threw the three of them on KP for the next Sunday.

This was bad enough for the Brooklyn Eagle. It was a blow to his pride. A greater blow came when the news of his sentence reached Acton Dennington Hawkins the

Third. Hawkins the Third came around to console the Eagle with the announcement that he—the terrible Acton D.—was temporarily mess sergeant. That was the last straw.

Private Warnke and Hawkins, since they first met, had reviled and belittled each other bitterly, played fiendish tricks on each other, fought anew the War Between the States—Brooklyn against Atlanta.

When the Brooklyn Eagle listened to the gloating taunts of the Pride of Peachtree Street, he tore the air with violent language. He cursed his fate and called upon heaven to have compassion upon his misery. He cursed the fair name of Georgia and he reviled the proud name of Acton Dennington Hawkins the Third, his ancestors and his progeny.

Came Sunday morning—first Hawkins and then the dawn. Private First Class (Specialist Second Class) Warnke was dragged from his warm bed at five-thirty and led, ranting and wailing, to the kitchen.

Acton the Third was in his glory. There were dishes for the Eagle to wash, floors for the Eagle to mop, back steps for the Eagle to sweep. The crowning ignominy for the Eagle came when his other favorite archenemy, Private John A. ("One-Shot") Bushemi, came upon him in the kitchen—peeling onions.

"Don't cry, Warnke," Bushemi cooed fiendishly. "Things are never as bad as they seem. And no matter how bad they are, weeping won't help them. No tears!"

"That's the end!" Warnke roared. "That's the absolute finish! Scum in the kitchen! Get this grinning throwback to the anthropoid out of here, Hawkins, or you'll curse the day! This shatter-pated slubberdegullion, this runagate urchin, this blacksheep son of Satan, this bumptious blot on the name of photography! Get him out or I leave myself!"

"Bushemi," purred the relentless Hawkins, "if you want a picture of the Eagle weeping into his onions, I'll keep him peeling until you get your camera."

Warnke rose with a hoarse shout, flung his knife into the onions and stalked to the mess hall, there to sit and glower. "This is what I get for being such a nice guy," he raged. "This is what I get for saving lives by not leapfrogging a convoy."

At lunch, life hit a new low for the proud Eagle. The grinning Bushemi, flanked by a corps of other idle-tongued hecklers, entered the mess hall and sat down to eat. The Eagle was a table waiter by this time.

"Hey, boy," they hooted, wallowing in his rising anger, "bring on more mashed potatoes! There's no more cake on this table, boy. Tell us, boy, about all them lives you saved. Haw haw haw!"

The Brooklyn Eagle held his peace. Except for an occasional withering glare at his persecutors, he held within him the heat of his righteous anger. The Eagle is a man who bides his time. Perhaps behind his massive brow lay thoughts of next Sunday, when Bushemi will take his turn at KP for having been caught sleeping at seven o'clock.

There should have been an immediate sequel to this, but there wasn't. The Pride of Peachtree Street went into seclusion at the end of the day and Private John A. ("One-Shot") Bushemi didn't come in that night until after the Eagle fell asleep.

Discretion is the better part of valor.

60. MAURY SHER, MY OLD BUDDY when we were together in the student cooks' battery, had been on an extended furlough. Before he returned, I had left on a three-day pass for Charlotte. We had not got together for two or three weeks, so I went over to his battery to look him up.

The battery street was almost empty; the mess-hall door was locked. The mess sergeant was nowhere to be seen. Finally I found a soldier who had seen Sergeant Sher in his room, so I looked for him there.

The sergeant lay on his lazy back on a stilted bunk in his cadre room, reading Dorothy Parker. The windows of the room had been equipped with flimsy green curtains, and partially deflated holiday balloons fluttered against them. On the wall above the bed hung a small oil painting of a forest, with an icy white mountain in the background. A writing table had been installed and on a shelf built in over his bunk were a reading lamp, a small radio, and a neat array of books.

I stood there surveying the place for a while. "What

in the sweet name of military hardship have you got here?" I asked him. "All this place needs is a couple of Morris chairs and a sign reading, 'What is home without a mother?' "

"Beginning to look nice, ain't it?" he said. "Just a few minor improvements here and there. Know where I can pick up a small upright piano at a good price?"

I looked over the room again and my eye fell on the resplendent forest scene. "Where'd you get this canvas knickknack? It's an original, isn't it?"

"It ain't nothing else but," he said. "Painted by a friend of mine up in Columbus. Guy knocks them off like that in about twenty minutes. How do you like it?"

"Aside from the fact that the waterfall is a little frothy and the mountain looks like something from a mentholatum advertisement, it would do credit to any mess sergeant's room in the whole Replacement Center."

"You didn't notice this," he said, lifting himself lazily from the bunk. From the table he took an ordinary-looking beer can with an extra lid on it. "John Bull Beer," he said. "Can't buy it anywhere except in my family's restaurants in Ohio and Pennsylvania."

He lifted the top lid, revealing a businesslike cigarette lighter. I took the can, struck the flint and a roaring blaze leaped at me. It burned merrily away.

"Not bad, huh? Good advertising scheme."

"It should come in handy," I told him, "any time the furnace goes blah. That little conflagration would heat a whole barracks in three minutes flat."

He twisted the dial of his radio and a high-pitched feminine wail bounced off the far wall. "I've been listening to the opera most of the afternoon—*The Magic Flute*."

"What happened to the magic skillet?" I asked. "How come you're lying around here instead of bustling about your kitchen—tickling the palates of the men with your culinary delights, as they say in the Army cooks' manual?"

"No supper tonight," he explained airily. "We're just changing cycles and there ain't nobody here but the noncommissioned officers, like myself. I told them to go and eat next door.

"This is the life, little man." He yawned. "Nothing to do, nothing to worry about. Just lie around, read and listen to the opera. Sans souci, as we French say—without care."

"Yeah," I sighed wearily. "And selt gornisht helfen, as we Jewish people say—nothing will help you, Maury, you're a disgrace to the tribe of Israel. They yank you into the Army to make a man of you—and now look at you. A softie. A sybarite. A lazy, good-for-nawthing ne'er-do-well. Is this industry?"

"Think nothing of it," he said. "I ain't wasting. I brought my car back from Ohio and I've got it rented out for the afternoon. I'm just lying here making money."

I looked at the boy silently and reviewed how our paths had parted. Here was Maury—Sergeant Sher now —a king of the kitchen, a plutocrat in an embroidered boudoir, a noncommissioned officer, a master of men. (The bum!) And here was I, who had abandoned a wonderful career as a cook to become what I was before I entered the Army—a hard-working, brow-beaten, hard-pressed, unthanked newspaperman.

Hargrove, I thought, selt gornisht helfen.

61. THE FIRST SERGEANT LOOKED OVER HIS GLASSES with a rather unpleasant gleam in his eye. He glanced significantly at the top of my head, so I removed my cap. The first sergeant adjusted himself in his chair and cleared his throat.

"Private Hargrove," he began slowly and deliberately, "the government of the United States, to whom no task seems impossible, has tackled the job of pulling you a little of the way out of your abysmal ignorance. With complete faith that heaven will help them in this job, they have begun a series of lectures about why you are being trained to fight, whom you are being trained to fight, and all the other little things you should know."

"Yes, sir," I said hesitantly, running my finger around the inside of my collar. "You mean the radio lectures on Tuesday and Thursday afternoons."

"From four until four-thirty," the first sergeant said. "The entire population has been invited by Upstairs to gather in the mess halls to hear and discuss these lectures. Yesterday afternoon you weren't on hand. Have you any last words before I pass KP on to you?"

"It's a rather long story, sergeant," I began.

"Here we go again," sighed the sergeant. "Have a chair and begin breaking my heart. It will make you feel better to have that off your chest before you go to the kitchen."

"Sergeant," I asked him, "were you ever editor of a high-school newspaper?"

"Is this long story about me or you?" the sergeant asked. "Please continue with your story."

"Well, sir," I continued, "only a high-school editor could know the pain that is in my heart. Only he could sympathize with me. I have gone back to my old job I had years ago. I am again a true high-school editor. I am editor of the Replacement Center section of the Fort Bragg *Post*."

"Meeting such a dignitary is one of the greatest occasions of my life," the first sergeant said dryly. "It is amazing how conversations can be switched around. When we started talking, you were explaining why you are being put in the kitchen police department."

"Sergeant, for days I round up news from battery reporters. There is always too much or too little. When there is too little, I have to write what is needed. When there is too much, I have to choose which battery reporter is going to horsewhip me for leaving his copy out."

"The chaplain is right up the street," the sergeant said.

"Then I have to edit all the copy, delete all classified military intelligence and take out all nasty cracks at first sergeants. Then I have to write headlines for all the stories and place them in whatever space I can find for them. Then I must draw everything up into pretty little pages. This is tedious and nerve-racking work."

"The chaplain will give you a sympathetic ear," the sergeant said. "I will give you only KP. Does anything you are saying relate to what we're talking about—why you weren't in the mess hall yesterday afternoon?"

"I was getting around to that, sergeant. On the day before the paper is issued, I have to go into Fayette-ville and keep a careful watch over the printers, to see that they don't put Third Regiment news on the Fourth Regiment page. If I am not there, they may even mix headlines and put church notices under 'Service Club Activities.' It is necessary that I be there."

The sergeant coughed. "I feel for you, Private Hargrove; I deeply sympathize. I wouldn't think of putting you on KP—"

"You wouldn't?" I gasped eagerly.

"Don't interrupt," the sergeant barked. "As I was saying, I wouldn't think of putting you on KP—if you hadn't committed a breach of etiquette by failing to RSVP the invitation. You didn't tell us you weren't coming. Or why."

My shoulders sagged. "Please don't keep the mess sergeant waiting," the top kick said. "He's expecting you now."

62. THIS MORNING'S MAIL BROUGHT A LETTER which somehow started my brain going through the winding course it takes and pushed it through to a startlingly sudden realization. The letter was from my old friend J. Milton Todd, Charlotte field representative of the Woodmen of the World, who used to drop in on me at the *News* occasionally with a news story or a dry joke.

It was a very pleasant letter, and I was still thinking about it when I went back to work after lunch. I couldn't estimate the number of news stories I've written about the Hornet's Nest Camp of the Woodmen. Hornet's Nest Camp No.— There I stopped. I couldn't remember the number that always went with the name of the camp in every story I wrote.

It was a trivial thing, but it started me thinking. Hugh White, the city editor, and I used to play a little game during slack periods of the day to test our memories. We'd quiz each other on the national numbers that go with the name of a fraternal organization in *News* stories. Mizpah Chapter No. 36, Order of the Eastern

Star; Hawthorne Grove No. 14, Supreme Forest Woodmen Circle; Charlotte Chapter No. 164, Women of the
Moose. I never missed them.

Now I can remember practically none of them. I
can't remember the names of the janitor's two assistants.

I'll admit that this sounds rather pointless, but it
isn't. It got me worried. I have a fairly good memory.
The only reason I could possibly find for forgetting so
much of what I was buried in seven months ago was
that all of that had been crowded from my mind. I
hadn't thought of any of it for months.

Great gods and little daffodils, I thought. Is Hargrove
becoming an Army man? Am I crowding everything
out of the picture except Army work and Army asso-
ciates and Army activities? Am I on the way to being a
thirty-year man?

I checked back through some old clippings of my
column, written during the first few weeks I was here.
Then I checked them with more recent columns. The
early ones, I found, were harmless enough at first
glance, but they carried throughout them a certain
undertone of genuine dislike for the work. There were
little sarcastic digs between the lines, weary and ironic
sighs.

Then the little digs began to grow weaker and
weaker. They were replaced by a more tolerant attitude
or, when I discussed something I didn't like, hearty
growls. Real old growls, bellyachers. It is an accepted
theory in the Army that the more a man gripes and
the louder he gripes the better he likes the Army.

The only decision I could make through studying the columns was that I seem to be adopting the philosophy of the old soldier. "If it's going to happen, it's going to happen, so why worry about it?" If I sleep until too late to stand reveille, I know that the first sergeant is going to put me on KP Sunday. The Sunday KP is an unpleasant thought—for next Sunday. But why worry about it?

I found that the noncommissioned officers whom I had looked upon as petty tyrants five or six months ago were, in my present opinion, all pretty good fellows. They have good common sense and most of them have a good sense of humor. The ones whom I actually disliked then, I still dislike.

When I first began going to Charlotte on occasional weekends, I always wore civilian clothes—"just to get out of the uniform and relax." I discovered when I returned from my New York furlough in November that I hadn't worn civilian clothes once during the trip. I never wear them now.

The thing began to worry me greatly. Finally, I went back to the darkroom, where Bushemi was mixing his hypo. I outlined the whole case to him.

"Bushemi," I asked him, "am I becoming a Good Soldier? Have I found a home here? Am I a potential thirty-year man?"

Bushemi hooted. "You're picking up in some ways. You shine your shoes and you keep fairly well in line. It might be conscientiousness, but it's more probable that you're just bucking for corporal. As for looking for a career in the Army, I can't see it in you. You're a born civilian, son. You're too fond of sitting up all night talking; you're too fond of sleeping late and eating at ungodly hours; you'll never be satisfied without a lot of fast action and civilian good times. You're too ambitious.

"You're a cocky son of a gun. You've got to be jawing back at everybody and everything. If it weren't for the emergency atmosphere and the knowledge of what you're in, you'd spend half your time in the guardhouse for insubordination. You're in no danger of becoming a lifetime soldier."

I thanked him and came back to the office. When Captain Winkel finished the work he was absorbed in, I was impressively busy on my afternoon's assignments. As Bushemi says, probably bucking for corporal.

63. HIS ADMIRING PUBLIC KNEW, when they saw him in the morning, that Thomas James Montgomery Mulvehill, private first class, was in fine form today. There was a brighter glint in his eye, a richer timbre in his golden Irish voice, a quicker grasp when he reached for his third serving of eggs at breakfast. It was quite evident that this was one of the Lieuthomas's busy days.

There was a swing to his walk when he came back to the barracks after chow. With more energy than was his usual wont, he went about his household chores. He threw his blouse into Bushemi's locker, his overcoat into mine, and last night's bath towel into Bishop's. He whistled brightly as he made his bed, and as he swept and mopped the floor he broke into his favorite song, " 'Tis the Same Old Shillelagh Me Father Brought from Ireland." Then he clapped his cap to the back of his massive head and strode briskly to work—on time!

Private Mulvehill's first five minutes were spent in quiet thought, in communion with his inner self, in contemplation of the "little deals" he planned to "swindle" during the day. Then he slammed on his cap, burst through the door and was gone. We saw him jump up and click his heels as he passed the post office.

Our first report on the Lieuthomas's activities came from one of the officers of the headquarters staff. "He came into my office to see if I had any news. While I was still trying to think of something, I found that he had already sold me a subscription to the camp newspaper and disappeared. It makes you dizzy!"

The next thing I knew, he had sprung out of nowhere, this fantastic Irish demon, and he had me by the lapel. "I was just talking to Miss Scarborough at the Service Club, McGee, and I think I can swindle a nice little deal for us there. She wants us to take over another program for her next Thursday evening, and if we can swing it right—boy, what a deal! Listen, chum, we can get a little time from one of the radio stations in Raleigh or Fayetteville and put on a little show that'll put us both on the big time. How would you like a second looey's commission in the Morale Branch?"

I was highly dazed by all this sudden opportunity for fame and fortune, but I replied that I was under contract to the Army of the United States and therefore not available for Broadway or the radio networks. I also explained that, although the prospect of becoming a second lieutenant sounded thrilling, I believed myself predestined to be a private. He was unimpressed. He was still determined to swindle the deal.

After he had come into the office fifteen minutes before lunch and dashed out six or seven pages of newspaper copy, he flew to the mess hall, where he cornered poor old Pope, the mess sergeant.

"Listen, McGee," I heard him saying to the cringing Pope, "I'm swindling a nice little deal now. Boy, are you lucky, McGee! I got eight beautiful young ladies who are playing in *Junior Miss* down at Center Theatre to agree to have supper here in your mess hall. Straight from Broadway, McGee, and they're going to eat supper with the lads in Headquarters Battery. We can swindle a swell deal with one of these charming and gracious young actresses at each of the first eight tables. Pictures in all the newspapers in the country. McGee, you're on the way to becoming the best-known mess sergeant in the whole United States!"

The Mighty Mulvehill did not join Bishop, Bushemi,

and me in our usual routine of fight-starting and trou
blemaking at lunch. Instead, we saw, he was at a table
with the battery commander, whom he was bedazzling
with a high-pressure monologue.

"We can swindle a nice little deal here with a battery
basketball team, captain," we heard him saying, "if
you'll just let us have a hundred dollars from the battery fund." A conversation started at our table, so we
couldn't hear the rest of it. We saw the captain shaking
his head in a very tired manner.

When the Lieuthomas returned to the barracks, Sergeant Hart was waiting for him. "The inspector said
your shoes were dusty this morning, Mule-hill. Too
dusty. He personally recommended you for KP next
Sunday."

Thomas James Montgomery Mulvehill slapped himself mightily on the forehead. "Great gods and rolling
mountains of sandstone!" he roared. "My shoes dusty?
What are they doing to me? What are they doing to
me? I'm crucified!" . . . .

He sank to his bed, a broken heap of shattered man-
hood. Private Mulvehill's busy day had died in its
youth. He was ruined for the rest of the afternoon. He
was incapable of swindling any kind of deal.

64. IN YEARS TO COME, when some angelic little grandniece climbs upon my creaking old knee and says, "Great-uncle, what did *you* do in the great war besides writing corny newspaper articles and being a father and a mother both to Mulvehill and Bushemi?" I will pat her golden curls and push her sunny little face in.

All through the great war, dearie, your old uncle was a very sick man.

The very first day your aged uncle spent in the Army, he was inoculated with the noxious venom of smallpox. That's the big round scar, child, just above the bottle gash. While the smallpox needle was still plunged to the hilt in my cringing flesh, my other arm was being impaled on a similar needle containing a horse-dose of typhoid fever. While this hellish virus was still raging through my tortured system, the man came around with pneumonia shots.

I remember, with considerable pain, that I was lending a hand to the mess sergeant the day they came looking for me to press my second typhoid injection upon me. I had been heaving big bags of potatoes at the rations depot. After the inoculation, I was so extremely ill (temperature 212) that the sergeant took mercy on me and let me wash pots for the remainder of the afternoon. There was no additional charge for the steam bath in which I luxuriated for hours.

On the third and last typhoid shot, I was helping the

mess sergeant again. I was washing pots this time. When he saw that I was at the point of death, he took pity on me once more and let me heave big bags of potatoes.

Incidentally, I was visiting a couple of weeks ago over at Hospital No. 2 and I ran across the old sergeant. He was being treated for a fractured ankle or something like that. Shortly after I left, he was being treated for a twisted arm and bruises about the throat.

Typhoid, terrible as it is, can't hold a thumbscrew up to the all-time wonder, tetanus toxoid. Two medical attendants pin you to the floor while a third assaults you with a hypodermic needle that looks like an air pump for Zeppelins. He sinks this into your arm and pours a quart or two of fiendish little lockjaw germs into your blood stream.

You walk away saying, "Well, that wasn't too bad." Then, suddenly, you fall to the floor in a dead faint. When you wake up, you look at your arm and discover the bicep you never suspected was there. The lump looks like one of these concrete mail-order air-raid shelters you see in the newspapers.

I was supposed to take three of those, three weeks apart. They waited four weeks for the third, so we had to start all over again. When I thought I was through with them—after five shots—they found that something had happened to my records. Take them over again!

By this time, I suppose, I had been given enough tetanus to wipe out the twelve tribes of Israel. There was more lockjaw in my arteries than there was blood.

Lockjaw Louie, I was knowed as. But I was brave—and wise. I took two more shots in series No. 3.

Then it was announced that we were to take yellow fever shots. This terrifying poison, it was stated, did not take its toll until five or six days after the injection. No other inoculations of any kind were to be mixed with yellow fever. My scheduled eighth and last tetanus injection would have to be postponed!

Can a man live with ten tetanus injections under his belt?

In quiet desperation I threw myself upon the mercies of the medical officer. "Pardon me," he said. "Did you say ten shots?" I explained that I had already had seven and I outlined the whole tragic story.

"This will never do," he said. "No man should be given so much tetanus toxoid. That stuff costs money. Three to a customer is quite enough. You may go, Private Hargrove, and don't come back!" That's how much my health and happiness means in a cold modern world.

In my autobiography, *Through Fire and Flood with the Bacillus Tetani,* I am still worried about what will happen in the chapter on yellow fever, tentatively titled, "The Mosquito in a Mechanical Age, or Will the Hypodermic Needle Ever Replace the Stegomyia Fasciata?"

But should I worry? Any yellow fever germ who manages to keep alive in these infested veins will have to wade through a mess of tetanus bacilli!

65. I WAS DOZING PEACEFULLY AT MY TYPE-
WRITER the other morning when there came a knock
on my elbow and a bright young voice shouted "Hey!"
at me. I looked up into the impish, cheerful, and un-
quenchably mischievous face of the boss's daughter,
Miss Sidney Winkel, age four. Miss Winkel was dressed
like the Navy and looked entirely too energetic for
such a drizzly morning.

"I'm to be the Valentine," she said, "and Johnny's
going to take my picture and you're to take me up to
the Service Club and carry Johnny's things for him and
wait for him to get there so you'd better put on your
jacket and cap and let's go."

No punctuation.

Much as I hate mawkish sentimentality and look
upon romance as idle foolishness for idle fools, there
was a certain determination in Miss Sidney Winkel's
voice. I rose slowly and donned my weather garments.
Miss Winkel then dragged me to the club.

"I'm going to have my picture taken with Spud
Parker," she said. Spud Parker is the general's son and
is considered quite an eligible bachelor by the younger
set.

"Is Spud Parker your boy friend?" I asked her
sleepily.

"Oh, no," she said. "Johnny and Tom Mulvehill and
Lieutenant Meek and Captain Wilson are my four best

boy friends but you're not my boy friend at all because you make faces and stick out your tongue and maybe if you could behave yourself you could be my boy friend."

"Pure fiddle-faddle," I told her. "I didn't ask to be your boy friend, anyway. I could have nine hundred hundred girl friends if I wanted to—prettier than you. Sticks and snails and puppy-dog tails, that's what girls are made of. So there."

Her only reply was an airy "myaaah," but you could see that she was affected. The old Indifferent Treatment always gets them.

"There's Tom in the cafeteria," she said. "Let's go see Tom."

Thomas James Montgomery Mulvehill, Pfc., was apparently making his morning rounds in search of news. He was, at the moment, engaged in his daily research in the Service Club's toast and coffee.

"Hello, sis," he said. "Hello, McGee. Pull up a chair. McGee, get the lady a drink. Something tall and cool. Such as a chocolate milk. What's the deal, sis?"

"I'm to be the Valentine," she said, "and Johnny's going to take my picture and old Hargrove has to take care of Johnny's stuff until Johnny comes and I don't like him anyway because he makes faces and sticks out his tongue and says sticks and snails and puppy-dog tails that's what little girls are made of and he's not my boy friend anyway."

"No punctuation," I said. I waggled my ears and stuck out my tongue at her.

"The next time I come," she said, "I'm going to bring some soap and every time he sticks out his tongue I'm going to put soap on it because it isn't nice to stick out your tongue." She emphasized her statement by paralyzing my wrist with her fist and sticking her tongue out at me.

"Let's have no unnecessary vibrations, McGee," said the Lieuthomas, looking up reproachfully over his glasses. "Coffee is five cents the cup." He beamed at her. She beamed back at him.

"I have seven boy friends," she said, raising one forefinger delicately and rubbing the other against it in a highly jeering gesture. "I have seven boy friends and you're not one of them and you're not anybody's boy friend." She hit me this time on the elbow and I made a horrible face at her.

"Myaaah," I said. "Who wants to be your boy friend anyway?"

"I wish you wouldn't blow smoke," she said. "It makes me cough and it's not nice to smoke anyway. Old cigarettes!"

I wearily crushed my last cigarette in the ash tray. "Woman, the eternal reformer," I sighed. "It wasn't like this in the Old Army."

Miss Sidney Winkel took off her sailor cap and arranged her big red hair ribbon. "You're a nasty old thing and you're not nice like Johnny and Tom and Lieutenant Meek and Captain Wilson and all my other boy friends," she said. After a pause she added, airily, "And Major Long and Captain Quillen, too."

"Myaaah," I sighed, wrinkling my nose violently.

"Oh there's Johnny," she suddenly cried, "and he's going to take my picture and—" She tripped off with a bewitching smile for Bushemi and a running line of babble.

"No punctuation," I said to Mulvehill.

"It's a woman's world, McGee," he said, reaching for another slice of toast.

66. "GET HIM AWAY FROM ME, BUSHEMI!" roared Private Thomas James Montgomery Mulvehill. "He's got that gleam in his eye. Get him away!"

"You're just being difficult, Lieuthomas," I told him. "Just sit down and relax." The Lieuthomas laid his enormous frame on the bunk and started slapping his knees in utter despair.

"What kind of deal are you trying to swindle this time?" he asked.

"Let's be reasonable, Private Mulvehill," I said, patting him reassuringly on the shoulder. "As you know, I am now working on Captain Winkel's sympathies to get a furlough sometime in February . . . the first half of February."

"I know what's coming," he screamed, "and I won't do it! I can't do it!"

"Now, as you know, furloughs are laden with little expenses—necessary little expenses. To help me along with the load, Sergeant Sher and Private Bushemi have already made philanthropic little loans. I have your name on my honor roll here, Lieuthomas. What's the donation?"

The Mulvehill cringed and edged away. "What do you need—from me?"

"Well," I estimated, "I should say that ten dollars would be a good sum for you. Shall I put you down for only ten dollars?"

"Great gods and refugee children," he gasped. "Ten dollars he says yet! Why don't you ask me for my life's blood? Six dollars he owes me already and now he's asking—oh, I can't stand it! I can't stand it! Take him away!"

Bushemi, Bishop, and I sat on the bunk across from him, waiting for his next move.

"My life's blood," he moaned. "Where's the six I lent you two months ago?"

"That was only five weeks ago," I reminded him gently, "and I've already paid two of that back. Three weeks ago I paid it back."

"Yeah," he protested, "but you borrowed it back the next day." He rose and paced the floor. "What are they doing to me? My life's blood they would draw from my veins! Thirty-six measly little dollars a month I make—and he wants ten dollars! Maybe I'm Winthrop Rockefeller. I should lend out ten dollars a clip! Thirty-six dollars, and he wants half!"

He paused in his pacing. "Thirty-six dollars. With laundry, thirty-four-fifty. With cleaning, an even thirty-two. This one I owe eight, this one three, this one four. From thirty-two take away fifteen. I've got seventeen dollars. He gets ten. I get seven. Phooey!"

"Thomas," I told him, "why didn't you tell me you had to borrow money last month? I am shocked. Next month you will not have to borrow money; I will see to that."

He bent his head and peered up from beneath a bushy eyebrow. "How."

"When the time comes that you are broke," I told him, "I will be owing you sixteen dollars."

"That's nice, ain't it?" he asked wearily.

"You see me, Lieuthomas, a sad and work-worn creature—an Alice-sit-by-the-fire whose only hope for the future is in the faint glimmering hope of a furlough. Day after day, week in and week out, I have worked my frail fingers to the shoulder blades to make things pleasant for you and Bushemi and Bishop. I have patched your quarrels with the mess sergeant. I have saved you from the terrible wrath of provoked Rebels. I have sat here at night, sewing buttons on my blouse so that you wouldn't have to wear it hanging open on your merry jaunts to town. Money could not pay for the things I have done for you and Bushemi. And now this. Ten dollars between me and spiritual starvation—and no ten dollars. How sharper than a serpent's tooth."

"Don't talk like that, Hargreen," he said, his voice cracking. "Put me down for ten."

I took the sheet of paper from my pocket and wrote his name on it.

The Mighty Mulvehill walked down the barracks aisle, muttering to himself about poverty and privation and where his money went to. He reached his bed and stood by it silently. Then he threw his arms wide in a gesture of mortal despair.

"I'm being crucified," he bellowed, and he fell, a crushed hulk of humanity, to his bunk.

67. THERE WAS A LITTLE NOTE STUCK IN MY TYPEWRITER when I came back from prowling for news. It looked like Private ("One-Shot") Bushemi's typing. "The stockholders of the Union of Hargrove's Creditors," it read, "will hold a business meeting this evening about seven o'clock in the latrine of Barracks No. 2, Headquarters Battery. Please be present or we will beat your head in."

It was the day before my furlough, so I got the general drift. The vultures who were contributing to the furlough would probably stand around frowning and figure out some sort of budget for my vacation. I could picture the blue-nosed demons slashing away at my enjoyment.

The meeting had an unexpectedly small attendance: Maury Sher, mess sergeant of Battery D of the Third and chairman of the ways and means committee of the Union; Private Bushemi, principal stockholder and president; and Private First Class Thomas James Montgomery Mulvehill, chaplain.

Private Mulvehill beamed. "Sergeant Hart sends his regrets. He has a heavy heavy in Lillington. He is with us in spirit, though."

"Come in, drip," said Bushemi.

Sergeant Sher got down to business. "I've got to hand it to you, son," he said. "Gone through this much of the month and still haven't tried to get any of your furlough money back from the chaplain! We're all proud of you."

"Shucks," I blushed. " 'Tweren't nothin'. I was able to bum a cigarette here and there."

"McGee," said Mulvehill, clearing his throat, "you leave tomorrow for New York, where there are many snares to trap the unwary. Don't buy any gold watches in the park or any stolen furs anywhere. You know, I presume, about buying the Brooklyn Bridge."

"Now, we don't have any restrictions about the way you use our money," said Bushemi. "Only last time you spent too much money on taxicabs. You'll have to use the buses and subways more this trip. All the shows you want to see, all the books you can buy—but taxicabs only for very special dates."

"Somebody has been exaggerating this taxicab—" I began.

"Taxicabs," Sher broke in, "only for very special dates. You may go to the opera once if you sit downstairs and twice if you sit in the Family Circle. You are not to buy more than six theater tickets. In uniform, you can see all the movies you want for two bits each."

"And be conservative in tipping the waiters," said Mulvehill, tapping his glasses on the window sill. "Very conservative. Short-change them, if necessary."

"Tell him about the budget," said Bushemi, with unnecessary impatience.

"As the matter stands on the furlough deal," said Sher, "you owe Bushemi 22 dollars, me 10, Mulvehill 10, Hart 10. That's 52 dollars. Counting the ten you'll wire Bushemi for before the week's over, it's 62. With what money we have taken from you and given to the chaplain during the past few weeks, you should make out all right."

"Must I be treated as a child?" I asked.

"Okay," said the sergeant, as if I had not spoken, "that's 62 dollars on the red side. Now, on the credit side, you have your wages of 42 dollars for February—minus a dollar and a half for laundry and a couple of bucks for cleaning. Debts that we can bank on your collecting on payday, 20 dollars. That's $58.50. From 62, take away $58.50, leaves three dollars and a half we ain't got."

"We can cut it down to size," I said wistfully. "I'll give you three and a half of my furlough money."

"Fit the income to the budget," said Bushemi, "never the budget to the income."

"I can get four dollars for my coin collection," I sighed.

"When you get back broke, McGee," said Mulvehill, "you are not to eat breakfast at the Service Club. You are not to take out any post exchange books. You will get your cigarettes from Sergeant Sher, who will ration them out to you as per budget."

"An allowance I've got now," I wailed. "Restrictions yet! This is a helluva way to go on a gay and carefree furlough! Why can't I be treated like a grownup?"

"Don't be difficult," said Bushemi. "We're just planning things for you. We are not restricting your pleasure. You go to New York, son, and have a good time with your ill-gotten gains. When you get back, you ain't got a thing to worry about."

"Is that all?" I asked, shoulders drooping.

"That's all, brother," said Sher.

"Except for the taxicabs," said Mulvehill. "Watch the taxicabs."

68. SERGEANT SHER, PRIVATE BUSHEMI, AND the other members of the Union of Hargrove's Creditors would have been quite pleased at the sight. Instead

of spending their money lavishly on taxicab sightseeing trips and expensive shows, I was dining quietly in a conservative grillroom with the Redhead. We weren't even discussing ways to spend their hard-earned money.

"Little man," she said, "will you please ask the waiter for more water?"

The waiter, a roguish-looking fellow with a sneaking twinkle in his eye, had been leaning against a post within spitting distance ever since we began dinner. He uncrossed his legs, straightened up, and grinned devilishly.

"I beg your pardon," he said, rather unctuously. "There is a fifteen million gallon shortage in water at this very instant. On the other hand, madame, all supply ships to Great Britain use Scotch whisky as ballast for the return trip. Perhaps madame would like a glass of Scotch whisky?"

The Redhead lifted an eyebrow. I lifted both shoulders.

"I wonder," she said, "what they use in the finger bowls here—rubbing alcohol? I do not want Scotch whisky. I want water."

"It is as madame wishes," the waiter said, bowing from the knees. He walked away and returned again to resume his position against the post. The Redhead drummed her fingers on the tablecloth. Having never learned the art of influencing waiters, I prepared to sit it out.

"Don't be afraid of him," said the Redhead. "Call his bluff."

"Ahem," I said. He stopped humming a little tune with which he had engaged himself, and he looked at we with kindly curiosity. "Ahem," I repeated. "Are you the waiter with the water for my daughter?"

He turned on a tight, polite little smile. "The water, monsieur, will be forthcoming. I have sent my friend Charles for the water."

The Redhead looked up, openly curious. "Your friend Charles, I take it, is the younger of the two and more capable of carrying a whole glass of water?"

The waiter shrugged his shoulders. "He is a timid man, madame. Why should I go for the water when he will get it for me? I am tired."

"You are a man of some astuteness," I ventured. "In the Army you would be a sergeant within two months."

"Perhaps I shall, monsieur. A month, two months, who knows? You are at Dix?"

"I am at Bragg," I told him. "I am at the Field Artillery Replacement Center, largest artillery training station in the world, Brigadier General Edwin P. Parker, Jr., commanding."

"I have a friend at the Field Artillery Replacement Center," he said. "He is in the Twelfth Battalion. You must look him up. I write his name for you on my card. You will give him the regards of Eduardo Enriquez?"

"The day I return," I promised him, "I shall look him up."

The timid Charles approached with the water, which

Eduardo poured for the Redhead. "This is too joyful an occasion for water, madame," he said. "A Martini?"

"Does Eduardo Enriquez personally endorse the Martini?" the Redhead asked.

"Eduardo Enriquez has been drinking them in the kitchen himself all evening," he beamed.

"I thought," said the Redhead, "that something more than music had soothed that savage breast."

"This is a joyful occasion," Eduardo crowed. "The three of us here together. If only one of us could have a birthday!"

Without a word, I produced three coins—a Nova Scotia penny and two dimes. The three of us odd-manned and Eduardo Enriquez was the odd man.

"Happy birthday, Eduardo Enriquez," said the Redhead. "Happy, happy birthday."

"We shall celebrate," he said, heaving a happy sigh. "In three minutes I shall be finished with my work. Will the noble artilleryman and the most beautiful redhead in all New York join me across the street at the bar where the Martinis are much better than here? It is the birthday of Eduardo Enriquez!"

I looked at the Redhead and she laughed quietly. Eduardo clasped his hands and gave us both a happy, dreamlike flash of a grin. "In three minutes—the three happiest people in New York will celebrate Eduardo's birthday." He rushed off, almost knocking another waiter down in his hurry.

"There's one thing about this town," said the Red-head. "You never know what to expect next."

69. PRIVATE JOHN A. ("ONE-SHOT") BUSHEMI WAS THE FIRST to welcome me back from my furlough. When the dawn whistle blew, Private Bushemi arose, placed his foot in the small of my back and jiggled until I awoke. He was decorated with his usual friendly grin, but a certain indefinable tragedy lurked behind it.

"Did you have a good time in New York, boy?" he asked. "Did you get the ten dollars I sent you?"

"I got the ten," I said, sticking a cautious foot out into the cold, "and I had as good a time as the law allows. What are you looking so unhappy about?"

"What did you do in New York?" he asked, ignoring the question.

"Monday night I went to see *Life with Father,* I told him, counting off on my fingers. "Tuesday night we celebrated a waiter's birthday; Wednesday night we went to see *Angel Street;* Thursday night we went to the Metropolitan to hear *Rigoletto;* Friday night the Redhead had influenza so I went alone to see *Macbeth.* What on earth is troubling you, Bushemi? You look actually pale."

"Did you like the opera, boy? Was it your first time at the Metropolitan Opera House? What kind of place is it? Real nice?"

"It's just the Saturday afternoon broadcast with the Great Golden Curtain and the Diamond Horseshoe thrown in," I said impatiently. "The Redhead tripped on a low aisle at intermission and almost fell on her face before Mrs. Cornelius Vanderbilt and everybody. We had good orchestra seats, too, creditors or no creditors. Tell papa what's on your mind."

"Is the Redhead very ill with influenza?" he asked, donning a look of concern. "Does she have influenza real bad?"

I sighed wearily. "The last time I saw her, she was lying on her deathbed with a horde of anxious relatives scurrying about spoiling her. She was enjoying herself immensely. There is something troubling you, Bushemi. Out with it!"

"Did you stop in Baltimore to see your grandmother? And how are your families in Washington? Has your kid brother been caught in the draft?"

"Bushemi," I said sternly, "this is so much beating about the temples and avoiding the issue. Who's been rocking your dream boat?"

"Well," he began reluctantly, "you know how Sher and Mulvehill and Hart and I went to such great pains to arrange your budget between furlough and payday."

"I'm painfully aware of it," I said. "I'm not to borrow any money before payday. I'm not to get any canteen checks, theater books, or barber tickets. I'm not to buy anything on credit and I'm to get your permission before I even send a uniform to the cleaner's."

"We had it figured out perfectly," he sighed. "We had it figured where you could pay my 32 dollars,

Mulvehill's 10, Sher's 10, and Hart's 10—all out of a 42-dollar paycheck—"

"With deductions in the pay, even," I said proudly.

"Hargrove," he said, "I don't know how to say what I have to say. I can't go on. I can't tell you. I can't ruin your perfect furlough."

"I know it has to do with the creditors," I said. "Go on."

He paced up and down between the bunks, biting his lower lip ferociously and slapping one hand upon the other. Then he sat down again.

"You know the pretty little payroll, where you write down 'Marion L. Hargrove, Jr.' beside your number so that you can get paid!"

"I signed it," I told him. "I distinctly remember signing it."

"When the Hargrovian creditors line up on payday to collect your pay," he moaned, "they're just going to have to stand there. The Union of Hargrove's Creditors has been red-lined."

I waited for the explanation.

"You signed it 'Marion Hargrove,' " he said, "as if it were an IOU. You don't get paid this payday. All of us will starve together."

You can't win.

70. THE JAPANESE ATTACK ON PEARL HAR-
BOR this afternoon came as stunning news to the men
at Fort Bragg. There had been a rumor, one day a
couple of months ago, that Germany had declared war
on the United States to beat us to the draw, and since
it was merely a rumor, there was no confirmation or
denial over the radio all day long. That supposed news
back then had been taken with a philosophic shrug and
the thought, "Well, it's what we've been expecting."

This today caused a different war feeling. It was not
what we had been expecting. To the soldiers here,
whose only attention to the newspapers is a quick
glance at the headlines, it was startling and dreadful.

The men who heard the news announcement over
the radio this afternoon at the Service Club were, for
the most part, new to the Army, with less than a month
of training behind them. Their first feeling of outrage
gave way to the awful fear that they would be sent away,
green and untrained and helpless, within a week.

The rumor mill began operation immediately. New
York and Fort Bragg will be bombed within the month,
the rumors said. Probably, by that time, all of us will
be in Hawaii or Russia or Persia or Africa. Green and
untrained and helpless. This business of teaching a man
for thirteen weeks in a replacement center will be dis-
pensed with, now that war is upon us. You're a civilian

one day and a rookie member of a seasoned fighting outfit the next.

Except for a few for whom the radio held a terrible fascination, the men thought first of communicating with their families, their friends, their sweethearts. They immediately went for writing materials and for the two public telephones of the club. Almost all of the 64,000 men of Fort Bragg were trying to reach their homes through the eight trunk lines which ran out of the pitifully overburdened little telephone exchange in Fayetteville.

Miss Ethel Walker, who was acting as senior hostess for the Replacement Center's Service Club, had planned an entertainment program for the evening, but when she looked out at the tension in the social hall, she despaired. She telephoned her boss, Major Herston M. Cooper, the special services officer.

"There's no use trying to put on the show tonight," she said. "Shall I cancel it? And may I turn off the radio?"

"If it's a good program, keep it," said the major. "And by all means leave the radio on. Just hang on; I'll be there in five minutes."

The major, a former criminologist and schoolteacher in Birmingham, was a lean and mischievous-looking infantry officer with a gift of gab and a camaraderie with the enlisted men. He sauntered into the Service Club, noised it about that he was going to talk, and hooked up the public address microphone.

"Here it comes," said an unhappy acting corporal. "Here comes the higher brass, to tell us the worst."

The major cleared his throat and looked over the crowd which gathered about him. "I know that this is your Service Club," he said, "and that I'm a staff officer barging in on you. Before I was an officer, I was an enlisted man. And, as an enlisted man, I've done more KP than any man in this room."

A little of the tension passed and the major lapsed into one of his conveniently absent-minded rambles. "In fact, I went on KP every time they inspected my rifle. Couldn't keep the thing clean."

He paused. "The main thing that has us worrying this afternoon is the very same thing we're being trained to protect. It's what they call the American Way—and they spell it with capitals.

"I have my own ideas about the American Way. I think the American Way is shown in you boys whose parents paid school taxes so that you could know what it was to cut hooky. It's shown in the men who pay two dollars to see a wrestling match, not to watch the wrestlers but to boo the referee. It's the good old go-to-hell American spirit and you can't find it anywhere but here.

"You and I both, when we were called into the Army, brought our homes with us. We've been thinking less about war than about getting back home after a while —back to our girls and our wives and our civilian jobs.

"Well, we know now where we stand and we don't have to worry about whether we're in for a long stretch or a short vacation. That should be cleared up now. We know that we've got only one job now and we haven't time to worry about the one at home.

"You're worrying because you're not prepared soldiers, you're not ready to fight yet. When the time comes for you to go, you'll be ready. You'll have your fundamental training before you leave the Replacement Center.

"Even if war is declared tomorrow, you'll be taught for a while here. And if war were declared tonight, we'd still have our Service Club and our movies and our athletics. During our off hours, we would. That's part of the American Way.

"Spending your duty hours at work and your leisure hours at worry—that's no good. That's what the enemy wants for you."

The major stopped again and looked at the soldiers seated at writing tables and the ones waiting for the telephones. "Someone once told me that the best thing to do with a letter you're not sure should be sent is to hang on to it for twenty-four hours. You might apply that to those letters you're writing now. I'm not going to write my family until tomorrow.

"Don't write or telephone home when you're under a strain like this. Your parents and friends are worrying about you now and there's no need to feed their worries. The letters most of you are writing are going to disturb your people back home, and they're going to write letters back that will react on you. Nobody's going to get anywhere like that.

"Relax for a while. Have a beer somewhere or get into a good argument or just go home and sleep it off. Then write home when you've had time to think it over. Let your letters be reassuring; you owe it to your folks.

"I guess that's all, boys."

He turned to leave the microphone, but returned as if he had suddenly remembered something.

"The regular variety show will go on tonight at eight o'clock," he said.

71. THEY COME AND THEY GO from the Replacement Center more quickly now, or perhaps it merely seems that they do. The training cycles have not been cut down much, but the turnover of men seems greater. Perhaps it's just that we notice the arrivals and departures more, now that war has given them grimness.

We call the train—the one that brings in recruits and takes out soldiers—the Shanghai Express. The term probably was used first by some disgruntled soldier who put into it the bitterness of a difficult transition from civilian to soldier. Now the term is used with a certain tender fondness by the permanent personnel of the Center, we who watch the men come and go.

The melancholy moan of a train whistle is heard in

the distance of the night and a sergeant clicks his teeth wistfully. "Here she comes, boys," he says. "Here comes that Shanghai Express." The sound of the whistle identifies all that touches the heart of a soldier.

There was a group of new men coming in this morning, down at the railroad siding. Their new uniforms hung strangely upon them, conspicuous and uncertain and uncomfortable—new uniforms on new soldiers.

They were frightened and ill at ease, these men. A week ago they had been civilians and the prospect of the Army had probably hung over some of them like a Damoclean sword. They had been told, by well-meaning friends, that the Army wouldn't be so bad once they got used to it. The Army will make you or break you, they had been told. The Army really isn't as bad as it's painted, they had heard. All of this, in a diabolically suggestive way, had opened conjectures to terrify the most indomitable.

This morning, they still hadn't had time to get over their fears. They still had no idea of what Army life was going to be like. Most of all and first of all, they wondered, "What sort of place is this we're coming into?"

Their spirits were still at their lowest point—past, present, or future.

The Replacement Center band, led by wizened little Master Sergeant Knowles, was there to greet them with a welcome that might dispel from them the feeling that they were cattle being shipped into the fort on consignment. First there were the conventional but stirring

military marches, the "Caisson Song" and all the rest.
And then there was a sly and corny rendition of the
"Tiger Rag," a friendly musical wink that said, "Take
it easy, brother."

A little reassured but still suspicious, the men went
from the train to the theater, where they would see a
program of entertainment and possibly hear a short
and casual welcoming address by General Parker.

This afternoon the sound of marching feet came up
Headquarters Street from the south and a battery of
departing soldiers approached. As they neared the headquarters building, there came the order, "Count
cadence—command!" and two hundred voices took up
a chant. They passed, counting their footsteps in ring-
ing ordered tones.

Laden with haversacks, they passed in perfect order.
Their lines were even, their marching co-ordinated and
confident. Their uniforms no longer bore the awkward
stamp. Their caps were cocky but correct and their
neckties were tucked between the right two buttons.

The cadence count is the scheme of the battery commander who feels proud of the men he has trained,
who wants to show them off to the higher-ups in Center
Headquarters. "The general might be standing by his
window now, watching my men pass," they say. "If he
isn't, we should attract his attention."

Just as their arrival marks an emotional ebb, their
departure is the flood tide. The men who came in a
few weeks ago, green and terrified, leave now as soldiers. The corporal whom they dreaded then is now

just a jerk who's bucking for sergeant. Although they are glad that they have been trained with other men on the same level here, the training center which was first a vast and awful place is now just a training center, all right in its way—for rookies. They themselves have outgrown their kindergarten.

The band is at the railroad siding, this time to see them off with a flourish. They pay more attention to the band this time. They know the "Caisson Song." They know their own Replacement Center Marching Song, composed by one of their number, a quiet little ex-music teacher named Harvey Bosell. They hum the tune as they board the Shanghai Express.

They see the commanding general standing on the side lines with his aide. He is no longer an ogre out of Washington who might, for all they know, have the power of life and death over them to administer it at a whim. He is the commanding general, a good soldier and a good fellow, and it was damned white of him to come down to see them off.

They board the train and they sit waiting for it to take them to their permanent Army post and their part in the war.

As a special favor and for old times' sake, the band swings slowly into the song that is the voice of their nostalgia, "The Sidewalks of New York." Yankee or Rebel, Minnesotan or Nevadan, they love that song.

You can see their faces tightening a little, and a gently melancholy look come into their eyes as the trombone wails beneath the current of the music.

Their melancholy is melancholy with a shrug now. Home and whatever else was dearest to them a few months ago are still dear, but a soldier has to push them into the background when there's a war to be fought.

With the music still playing, the train pulls slowly out and Sergeant Knowles waves it good-bye with his baton.

An old sergeant, kept in the Replacement Center to train the men whose fathers fought with him a generation ago, stands on the side and watches them with a firm, proud look.

"Give 'em hell, boys," he shouts behind them. "Give 'em hell!"